WALKS FOR ALL AGES

G000061156

SOMERSET

SUE ROBINSON

BRADWELL
BOOKS

WALKS FOR ALL AGES

SOMERSET

SUE ROBINSON

BRADWELL
BOOKS

Published by Bradwell Books

9 Orgreave Close Sheffield S13 9NP

Email: books@bradwellbooks.co.uk

© Sue Robinson 2013

1st Edition

ISBN: 9781902674520

Print: Gomer Press, Llandysul, Ceredigion SA44 4JL

Design by: Erik Siewko Creative, Derbyshire
eriksiewko@gmail.com

Photograph Credits: © Sue Robinson
Page 7 © Shutterstock. Mike Charles 2013
Page 16/17 © Shutterstock. Liliya Sayfeela Trott 2013

Maps: Contain Ordnance Survey data © Crown copyright and database right 2013

CONTENTS

INTRODUCTION

The County of Somerset.

Somerset is a county of contrasts and has three Areas of Outstanding Natural Beauty: the Quantocks, the Mendips and the Blackdowns. Two-thirds of the National Park of Exmoor is located in the county and it offers the visitor wonderful scenery of the moors, the river valleys and the beautiful coastline.

Somerset gets its name because of the varied landscape, and was known as "the land of the summer people". Prehistoric farmers worked on the hills during the winter and grazed their animals on the lush grass on the Levels during the summer. The wetlands of the Somerset Levels, which are predominantly below sea level and are subject to flooding, are rich in flora and fauna, and in the winter are visited by many wading birds.

The coastline offers everything from cliff-top walks to miles of sandy beaches and offshore islands. The Bristol Channel has the second highest tidal rise in the world. There are small coastal villages as well as Victorian resort towns with elegant piers. There are also a number of holiday parks and resorts along the coastline which many visitors enjoy.

Taunton is the largest town in Somerset and is the administrative centre for the county. Many of the towns are steeped in history. The Romans traded in lead, which they found in the Mendip Hills, developing the city of Bath as a famous spa resort. Many of the smaller towns were established on the cloth and wool industry in medieval times.

There are many ruined castles to be found and impressive early manor houses, together with the well-known Georgian buildings of Bath. Somerset is a very pleasant place and there is always something more to discover.

LORNA DOONE VALLEY

This beautiful walk takes you along the Doone Valley and Badgworthy Water, and then there is a gentle climb out of the valley with wonderful views of the surrounding area and on to Oare Church.

The stony tracks are wide with paths across fields. There are no stiles. It can be muddy in wet weather. Parking is at the Lorna Doone Farm car park, Malmsmead approached off the A39 near Lynmouth.

Oare Valley Vista

The village of Oare is situated on the border or Somerset and Devon in the Exmoor National Park. It is said that Lorna Doone Valley and Badgworthy Water is where RD Blackmore located, and was inspired to write, his novel Lorna Doone, a romantic tale about two rival families who lived on the moor. Blackmore, who lived in London, used to come and stay with his grandfather, who was the Rector of Oare, and who would tell him stories of the families who lived locally.

Oare Church

Oare Church of St Mary's has been a parish church for at least eight hundred years. In RD Blackmore's novel he portrays Lorna being shot on her wedding day to John Ridd by Carver Doone through a small window at the end of the church. Luckily Lorna survives the shooting and goes on to marry John Ridd at a later date.

Exmoor National Park is small and compact with contrasting beautiful landscapes and is ideal for families to tour and explore. Exmoor offers the visitor both moors and wooded valleys as well as a magnificent coastline bordering the Bristol Channel. Two-thirds of the National Park is in Somerset and one-third in Devon.

Badgworthy Water

Lorna Doone Farm

THE BASICS

Distance in miles and km: 3 miles (5km)

Gradient: Wide level track with one incline.

Severity: Easy, a gentle incline.

Approx min time to walk: 1½ hours.

Stiles: None.

Maps: OS Explorer OL9 Exmoor.

Path description: Wide stony and grass tracks, field paths.

Start Point: Lorna Doone Farm car park, Malmsmead GR 791 477.

Parking: Lorna Doone Farm car park.

Dog friendly: On leads.

Public Toilets: In car park.

Nearest food: Cafe Deli, Lorna Doone Farm.

LORNA DOONE VALLEY WALK

1. The walk starts from Lorna Doone Farm car park, Malmsmead and you leave the car park heading towards Lorna Doone Farm and shop. You then take the road to your right following the direction sign 'Lane leading to Public Footpath Doone Valley', follow uphill to where the road curves right and go straight on through a gate to the left.

2. You continue to follow the track for approximately 1 mile (1.6km) with Badgworthy Water on your left-hand side until you reach a memorial stone for RD Blackmore. Here you then turn and retrace your steps back along the track, with the river now on your right-hand side, until you reach a wooden bridge which crosses the river and you enter a field, which is a camping site at Cloud Farm. Continue straight ahead towards a red phone box and wooden signpost.

3. You then follow the hard track bearing to the left towards the farm buildings and continue into and through the farm building; here you will see a metal farm gate. Continue through the farm gate and follow the track ahead, which takes you up towards another gate. Stop to take in the wonderful views of the valley. Continue through the gate following a grassy track as it bears uphill and to

the right. At the top of the hill you meet another gate. Go through the gate and continue ahead on a grass track, following it as it bears around to the right and another gate is ahead of you. Go through the gate and follow the track as it bears to the left and keeping to the left down the slope to another

Bridge Over Oare Water

gate. Go through the gate and continue down the grass track, with the fence on your left-hand side, to reach a gate and road. Oare Church can be seen on your left-hand side.

4. Turn left on the road and the entrance to Oare Church is on your left. After visiting the church you turn left onto the road and immediately right (signposted Lynmouth/Porlock), continuing along the road which crosses the bridge over Oare Water. As the road curves to the left follow the footpath sign on your left, marked Malmsmead.

5. Go through the gate and follow the grass track across field to a gate.

Fingerpost
Footpath
Cloud Farm
Doone Valley ½
Bridleway
Oare ¾

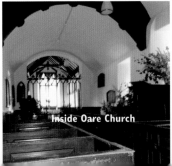
Inside Oare Church

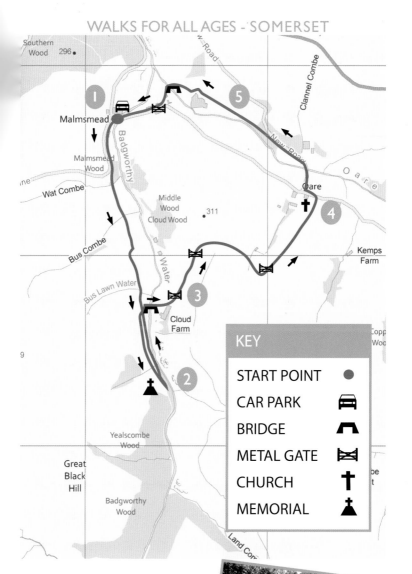

KEY

START POINT	●
CAR PARK	🚗
BRIDGE	⌒
METAL GATE	⋈
CHURCH	✝
MEMORIAL	▲

Continue through a series of gates, passing Oaremead Farm on your left. At the last gate by a wooden signpost you turn left along a track between two hedges to meet Oare Water. Turn right and cross over a footbridge. Continue up the track to pass through a gate and ahead to the road, where you turn right. The road then takes you past the entrance to Cloud Farm and back to Lorna Doone Farm.

DUNSTER CASTLE

An interesting and scenic 4-mile (6.5km) circular walk on undulating landscape. Bat's Castle is an Iron Age Hill Fort on a summit of a 692ft (210m) hilltop. Spectacular 360-degree panoramas of Exmoor and the coast can be seen.

Dunster Castle

The route takes you through Dunster Deer Park along field paths and stony tracks with some uphill climbs. When wet the fields can be muddy. Parking is at the Gallox Bridge car park via Park Street from A396.

Dunster is situated in the Exmoor National Park which has a landscape of great variety and covers 267 square miles (692 sq km) of Somerset and Devon. The magnificent Dunster Castle is a former motte and bailey castle, now a country house. The Castle lies on the top of a steep hill called the Tor, and has been fortified since the late Anglo-Saxon period. In the 11th century, William de Mohun constructed a timber castle on the site as part of the pacification of Somerset.

A stone shell keep was built on the motte by the start of the 12th century. At the end of the 14th century the Castle was sold to the Luttrell family, who continued to occupy the property until the late 20th century. In 1976 the Castle and all its land was given to the National Trust and it is open to visitors.

The walk you will follow is in the Dunster Forest Crown Estate. The lands belonging to the castle were sold to the Crown in 1950 and cover over 9,000 acres. The land consists of the most beautiful countryside with forests, woodlands heaths and agricultural land. There are numerous paths and trails across the estate. Bat's Castle is one of the larger Iron Age hill forts on Exmoor.

It is unusual as it has a ditched causeway projecting outwards from the entrance.

Woodland track

There are a number of outlying ditches to the south-east which may have been dug when the fort was used as a camp in the Civil War. When reaching the fort you will be amazed by the magnificent views of the Bristol Channel, Minehead, and even as far as the Welsh Coast on a clear day.

The medieval Deer Park through which you walk was landscaped for the Luttrell family in 1755 in its present position to enhance the castle grounds. The park supplied venison and other game for the castle. Fallow deer can still be found in the area but are not confined to the park boundaries.

Withycombe Hill

Bats Castle Circuit 4 miles

Deer Park Circuit 3 miles

National Park Centre *i*

THE BASICS

Distance in miles and km: 4 miles (6.5km)

Gradient: Undulating with one main uphill climb

Severity: Easy, One steep climb and gradual descent

Approx min time to walk: 2 hours

Stiles: No stiles

Maps: OS Explorer OL9 Exmoor

Path description: Pavements, tracks, open countryside, can be muddy

Start Point: Public car park at Gallox Bridge GR 989 432

Parking: Public car park via Park St. From A396 at Gallox Bridge GR 989 432

Dog friendly: On leads

Public Toilets: In village

Nearest food: Various restaurants and cafes in village

DUNSTER CASTLE MAP

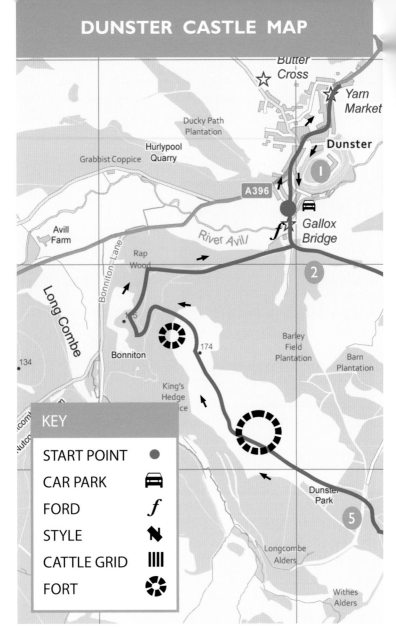

KEY

START POINT	●
CAR PARK	🚗
FORD	*f*
STYLE	✖
CATTLE GRID	‖‖
FORT	✳

1. From the car park turn left and walk between the cottages towards Gallox Bridge. This medieval packhorse bridge was the lowest crossing of the River Avill, which was tidal up to this point. Gallox Lane, which crosses the bridge, meets other ancient roads which were used to cross the bridge to Dunster. Cross the bridge and continue ahead in the direction of Dunster Forest Crown Estate, passing a thatched cottage on your right.

2. On reaching the information board go through the kissing gate and follow the signpost reading 'Carhampton one mile'. You are slowly ascending through the

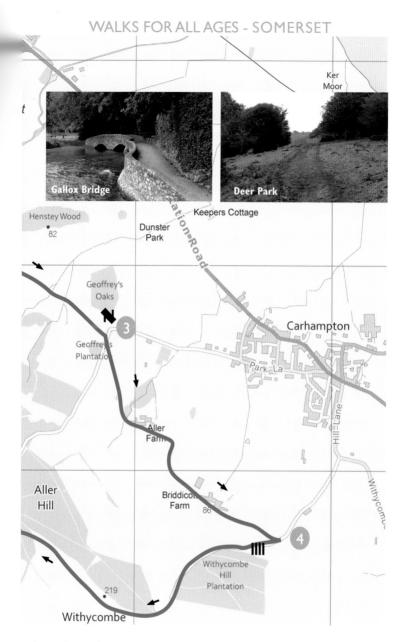

Gallox Bridge

Deer Park

deer park and after a few hundred yards join a fence line on your left. As you ascend there are good views of Dunster Castle to your left. Continue uphill and then drop down to pass through a gate/ hunting gate and then continue to follow the fence line to the brow of the hill to pass through a gate and immediately reach Park Lane (a track).

3. Take the footpath across the lane and over a stile into a field. Cross diagonally (south-eastwards) aiming for the gap in the far hedge, to the right of a barn at Aller Farm. Follow the grassy track ahead between barns, and where the track bends

3 Cont.

sharp left turn right through a gate into a field, and then sharp left to walk with the hedge on your left. Pass through a gate and turn right to follow the hedge to pass through a further gate and then go half left to a track which takes you through several gates to pass through the farmyard of Briddicott Farm.

4. You reach a road in front of the farmhouse and where it bends sharp left continue straight on following a track between barns and then between hedges. You join Hill Lane (a track) at a T-junction and turn right, walking steadily uphill until you reach a cattle grid. Keep on uphill into more open country with gorse and join another track coming in from your left. This is the Macmillan Way West. (The Macmillan Way is a long-distance footpath from Boston in Lincolnshire to Abbotsbury in Dorset. The proceeds of the walk book go to the Macmillan Cancer Relief charity.) It will be followed back to Dunster, which is signposted (2.5 miles). Past the signpost follow the track ahead to go over the top of Withycombe Hill, keeping to the edge of the conifer plantation to your right.

5. Arrive at a gate into the plantation and continue straight ahead and almost immediately you reach a Y-junction where you take the right fork to come to a major path junction at Withycombe Hill Gate. Here turn left through the large gate, following the bridleway to Dunster. Continue uphill (ignoring footpath to Dunster on right) past Bat's Castle and you now start to descend. Continue to descend and follow the Bat's Castle Circuit signposts; this will take you back to Gallox Bridge and Park Street car park.

Watermill at Dunster

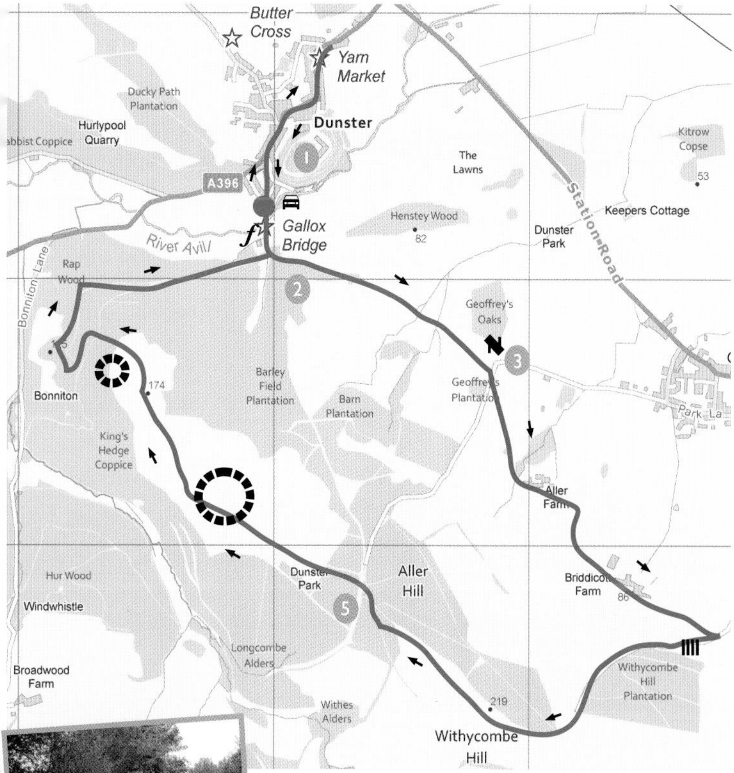

Butter Cross

Yarn Market

Ducky Path Plantation

Hurlypool Quarry

Rabbist Coppice

Dunster

The Lawns

Kitrow Copse

53

Keepers Cottage

A396

Station Road

River Avill

Gallox Bridge

Hensley Wood
82

Dunster Park

Rap Wood

Bonniton Lane

Geoffrey's Oaks

174

Bonniton

Barley Field Plantation

Barn Plantation

Geoffrey's Plantation

Park Lane

King's Hedge Coppice

Aller Farm

Hur Wood

Windwhistle

Dunster Park

Aller Hill

Briddicott Farm
86

Broadwood Farm

Longcombe Alders

Withes Alders

219

Withycombe Hill

Withycombe Hill Plantation

EAST QUANTOXHEAD, KILVE

This gentle walk takes you across open countryside and along the beautiful coastal path with wonderful views over the Bristol Channel, starting from the quiet village of East Quantockhead.

There are opportunities to go fossil hunting on the beach at Kilve and visit two very interesting churches at Kilve and East Quantoxhead. Parking is at 'The Court Car Park', East Quantoxhead, which can be found off the A39 near Kilve.

The Quantock Hills is a range of hills west of Bridgwater in Somerset. The range runs from the Vale of Taunton Deane in the south, for about 15 miles (25km) to the north-west, ending at East Quantoxhead and West Quantoxhead on the coast of the Bristol Channel, and was England's first Area of Outstanding Natural Beauty.

East Quantock village appears to be caught in a time capsule, with its exquisite manor house, thatched cottages, medieval barns, its own duck pond and old mill building. The manor house known as The Court House has been the home of the Luttrell family for seven and a half centuries. The small church of St Mary's lies close to the manor house wall, and has fantastic woodcarvings. The small church has a close association with the Luttrell family and, inside, there is the 16th-century tomb of Sir Hugh Luttrell. The church was built in its present position because of the risk of flooding in early times. It is built of locally quarried grey lias and granite.

Kilve lies at the northern end of the Quantocks and is a picturesque village consisting of three settlements. Here you will find the ruins of the old Chantry, founded in 1329 and once used for storing barrels of spirits smuggled in to Kilve Pill. The beach is a Site of Special Scientific Interest and a favourite haunt of geologists with its spectacular rock formations and fossils. Kilve has the remains of a red-brick retort built in 1924 after the shale in the cliffs was found to be rich in oil.

Kilve Beach

The Shaline Company was founded in 1924 to exploit these strata but was unable to raise sufficient capital. The company's retort house is thought to be the first structure erected here for the conversion of shale to oil and is all that remains of the anticipated Somerset oil boom.

Rock form at Kilve Beach

THE BASICS

Distance in miles and km: 3 miles (5km)

Gradient: One slight uphill

Severity: Easy walking with one slight uphill

Approx min time to walk: 1½ hours

Stiles: No stiles

Maps: Os Explorer 140 Quantock Hills and Bridgewater

Path description: Tracks, field paths and cliff tops

Start Point: Court House Car Park, East Quantoxhead. GR 137 435

Parking: Court House Car Park, East Quantoxhead. GR 137 435

Dog friendly: On leads

Public Toilets: None on route

Nearest food: Cafe at the Chantry, Kilve

1. The walk starts from East Quantoxhead village at 'The Court Car Park'. Walk across the car park towards the church and kissing gate. Go through the gate and follow a path that bends to the left towards a farm gate. You may wish to visit St Mary's Church at this point. You then continue across the field to a further farm gate and road. Turn right on the road and walk along the road and where the road bends to the left take the grassy lane to the right.

2. Climb steadily up the lane to reach a kissing gate and farm gate on your right. Go through the gate and follow the permissive field path with the hedge on your right. Here there are wonderful views of the Bristol Channel and the Welsh Coast ahead and to your left you can see Minehead and Exmoor. You continue to follow the field path over two further fields and through two more kissing gates down to the cliff top.

3. The open cliff-top path continues down towards a dip with a ruined lime kiln on your right. This was built in about 1770 to process limestone, which was shipped from Wales to make into lime for fertiliser and mortar. Here you bear right to cross the dip and then bear left to follow the cliff-top path. Take note of the cliff's alternating layers of blue-grey lias and grey shale. Continue along the cliff-top

The Court Entrance

path with a wire fence on your right, with the old Tudor Court House also in view. You will reach a kissing gate which takes you to a tarmac path and open grassy area and Kilve Beach.

4. Continue along the tarmac path towards red brick chimney which was an old oil retort house used for oil distillation from 1924. There is oil in the grey shale but it is far too difficult to extract. Follow the path through the Kilve car park and along the road past the old Chantry to the Church of the Virgin Mary on your right.

5. Go through the church lychgate and keep to the left of the church to a kissing gate. Go through the gate and follow the

St Mary The Virgin Church

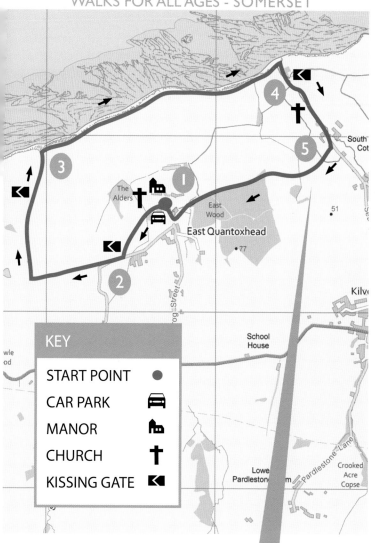

KEY

START POINT	●
CAR PARK	🚗
MANOR	🏠
CHURCH	✝
KISSING GATE	◖◗

farm track ahead, crossing over a small bridge by a stream and across three fields to a kissing gate and farm gate. You are now on a stony track which bears right and left and takes you back into the village of East Quantoxhead by the village pond and the Court House car park.

TAUNTON RIVER TONE

This is an easy level walk which starts in the centre of Taunton and takes you along the banks of the River Tone and across the water meadows to Longaller.

Taunton is the county town of Somerset. The town, including its suburbs, has an estimated population of 61,400. It is the largest town in the county of Somerset. The town has over 1,000 years of religious and military history and is surrounded to the west by Exmoor National Park, while to the east are the Quantock and Brendon Hills. Travelling south you have the Blackdown Hills and to the north you reach the coastline of

Enclosed Path

the Bristol Channel, the towns of Minehead and Weston-super-Mare and the Mendip Hills. The low-lying wetlands of the valley are an important area for wildlife and are known as the Somerset Levels.

Longaller Mill

Taunton Castle originated in the Saxon period and was the scene of the "Bloody Assize" when Judge Jeffreys tried over 500 supporters of the failed Monmouth Rebellion in 1685. The remains of the castle now house the Museum of Somerset with the famous hoard of Roman coins which were found near Frome in April 2010. The Frome Hoard contains 52,503 Roman coins found by metal detectors. The coins were contained in a ceramic pot 18 inches (45cm) in diameter, and date from AD 253 to 305. The hoard is one of the largest ever found in Britain, and was officially valued at £320,250. Entry to the museum is free.

The River Tone is about 32 miles (51 km) long. It rises at Beverton Pond in the Brendon Hills, and is dammed at Clatworthy Reservoir. The reservoir outfall continues through Taunton and Curry and Hay Moors, which are designated as a Site of Special Scientific Interest. Finally, it joins the River Parrett at Burrowbridge and then flows out into the Bristol Channel at Burnham-on-Sea.

The river passes through the centre of Taunton under the magnificent North Bridge, also known as the Tone Bridge,

River Tone

which was constructed in 1895 and includes globe lamps which are thought to be part of the earliest electric street lighting scheme in a British town. In the 17th century an act of parliament agreed that the river could be made navigable, but when the Bridgwater and Taunton Canal was built in 1872, which made navigation much easier, the river deteriorated and was no longer used for navigation.

Longaller Mill

Goodlands Gardens

THE BASICS

Distance in miles and km: 4 miles (6.5km)

Gradient: Flat

Severity: Easy level walking

Approx min time to walk: 2 hours

Stiles: 3 stiles

Maps: OS Explorer 128 Taunton Blackdown

Path description: Metallic footpaths and field tracks

Start Point: Car Park, Castle St or Enfield Car Park GR 226 244

Parking: Castle Street or Enfield Public Car Park GR 226 244

Dog friendly: On leads

Public Toilets: Taunton Centre, French Weir Recreation Ground

Nearest food: None on route, Taunton Town Centre

TAUNTON RIVER TONE MAP

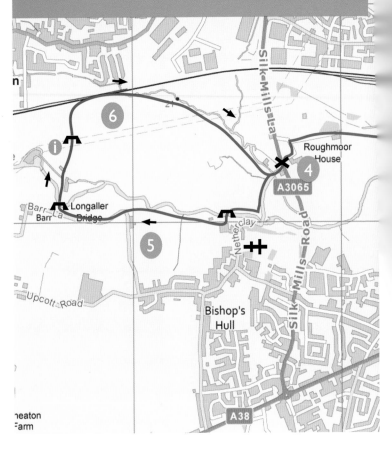

1. Leave the car park and turn to your right, and after a short distance cross the road and take the first turning on your left, walking past the bus station towards Castle Green with the Castle Hotel ahead of you. On your left are Taunton Castle and the Somerset Museum. To your left take the glass-lined pathway beside the Castle and then cross over the footbridge ahead of you into Goodlands Gardens. Turn right along the path to a further bridge, and go left across this wooden bridge spanning the River Tone.

2. At a fingerpost showing directions to French Weir turn left and follow a tarmac path along the side of the river. The footpath then enters Clarence Street, in which you continue left, and the footpath takes you into French Weir recreation ground. Continue to follow the footpath beside the river to the weir and around to the right, passing a toilet block, until you reach the corner of the recreation ground and a narrow path with a signpost marked 'Two Counties Way'.

3. Continue to follow this path with the river on your left until you reach a wooden ramp. Take a look at the Willow Cathedral built in Longrun

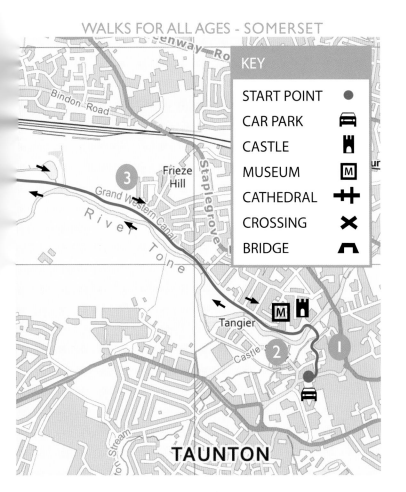

KEY

START POINT ●
CAR PARK 🚗
CASTLE ♜
MUSEUM Ⓜ
CATHEDRAL ✝
CROSSING ✕
BRIDGE ⌒

TAUNTON

Meadow to your left if you wish, but your route takes you down the ramp and you follow the riverside path. At the end of the field the path bears around to the right towards a small wooden bridge. Cross the bridge and turn left and follow the hard track with a small lake on your right as it winds through this open park area. Ignoring the first path which bends in from the right, continue on the track and just before you reach the second path coming in from the right turn left along a short grassy path onto a farm track. Turn right along the farm track, passing the large white house of Roughmoor Farm,

and follow the high-hedged lane to meet a T-junction. Here you turn left and follow the road around to meet the busy main road.

4. Take care crossing this busy road and continue along the lane 'Netherclay' until you meet a weak bridge and 'The Old Mill' house. Go through the gate to your right and follow the field path beside the River Tone until you reach a small bridge by an information board on your left. Cross over the bridge and turn right and follow the enclosed lane which winds between old buildings. The river is now on your right. You then

4 Cont.

reach a stile which you cross and then follow the field path alongside the river and through a gap into the second field following the path, with the hedge on you left, until you reach a stile and farm gate on your left.

5. Turning right onto the road, walk along this country lane, taking the second turning on your right signed 'Longaller Mill'. Passing Longaller Mill and crossing Longaller Bridge, go through the kissing gate ahead of you into the field. Follow the field path with the hedge on your left and then continue ahead across the field following the path to a stile ahead (ignoring a stile on your right). Over the stile, cross the field heading towards another stile and metal railway bridge. On reaching this stile do not go over the stile but turn sharp right along the field path ahead, following alongside the railway.

6. Continue to follow the path over fields next to the railway line and then Norton Brook on your left before reaching a metal kissing gate and road. You are now back in 'Netherclay'; turn left and retrace your route back to Taunton following the River Tone.

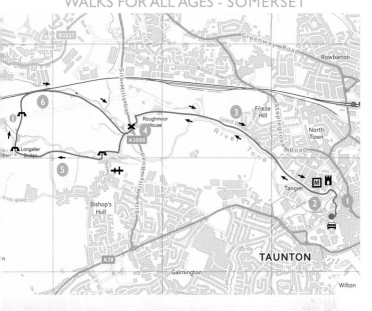

BRIDGWATER CANAL

A 4-mile (6.5km) circular walk along the banks of the Bridgwater and Taunton Canal and beyond. This easy flat walk is along the canal towpath through villages and across fields on the Somerset Levels.

Children will enjoy the fun of finding the sculpture stones representing the planets placed along the canal towpath and visiting the large sculpture of the Sun at Higher Maunsel Lock. Park at the Canalside car park at Maunsel Lock near North Newton, which is found signposted off the A361 at West Lyng.

Bridgwater Canal

The area around Maunsel and North Newton, two of the villages in the parish of North Petherton, is known as the Garden of Eden because of the fertile land below the Quantock Hills.

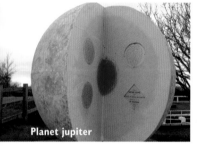
Planet jupiter

The Somerset Levels are bisected by the Polden Hills and are drained to the south by the River Parrett and to the north by the Rivers Axe and Brue. The Mendip Hills separate the Somerset Levels from the North Somerset Levels. The area supports a vast variety of plant and bird species and is an important feeding ground for birds. The Levels and Moors include 32 Sites of Special Scientific Interest, of which 12 are also Special Protection Areas. A lot of the land is below sea level and is subject to flooding, but this is managed by a number of drains and rhines so that it can be farmed all year round. The Somerset Levels is an important area for tourism with many places of interest for the walker and cyclist.

The Bridgwater and Taunton Canal was opened in 1827 to link the River Tone with the River Parrett, but shortly after its opening the railway from Bristol to Exeter arrived, so the canal went into decline. It was later purchased by the railway, which kept the structure in good order, and it was restored by Somerset County Council as a leisure facility and re-opened in 1994. The canal is now

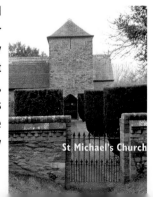
St Michael's Church

maintained and managed by The Canal and Water Trust.

The canal is home to the "Somerset Space Walk", a scale model of the Solar System centred on the "Sun" at Maunsel Lock with the planets located along the towpath in both directions. The Space Walk was designed by a local man, Pip Youngman, in order to demonstrate the scale of the Solar System in an interactive way. The inner planets are grouped around the Sun, and each of the plinths doubles up as a milestone showing the distance from Bridgwater to Taunton.

Maunsel House is a 13th-century manor set in 100 acres of parkland and is a venue for weddings and special events. The house has been in the Slade family since 1771 and it is said that Chaucer wrote The Canterbury Tales whilst staying at Maunsel House.

THE BASICS

Distance in miles and km: 4 miles (6.5km)

Gradient: Flat

Severity: Easy

Approx min time to walk: 2 hours

Stiles: Two Stiles

Maps: OS Explorer 140 Quantock Hills and Bridgwater.

Path description: Canal towpath, quiet lanes and field paths

Start Point: 'Canalside' Maunsel Lock TA7 0DH

Parking: Canalside car park, Maunsel Lock GR 307 298

Dog friendly: On leads

Public Toilets: Maunsel Lock at start of walk

Nearest food: Canal cafe at start open April- October

BRIDGEWATER CANAL

1. The walk starts from the Canalside car park at Maunsel Lock, leaving the car park and turning left over the bridge and immediately left along the canal towpath. Continue along the towpath, passing a long row of poplars, until you reach bridge No. 16. Leave the canal now and go up onto the road. Turn left over the bridge, crossing the canal, and continue along this quiet road, passing Turners Farm on your right, before reaching a road junction.

2. Turn left and continue along the lane, passing the entrance to Maunsel House. On reaching the old brick barns on your right you can take the short track next to the barns to view the quaint St Michael's Church, part of the Maunsel Estate. Retrace your steps and continue along the lane, passing the old Corn Mill on your right and ignoring the footpath sign on your left. Continue past the pink 'Mill Farmhouse' on your left to reach immediately a drive to house on your left and go through gates and left across the garden lawn to a wooden ramp and kissing gates. You then walk diagonally through the walnut grove, heading towards farm buildings in the distance, to find a stile.

3. Climb over the stile, turn right and continue along this lane to a road junction. As the road bends to the right, go left along the lane towards Hedging. At the T-junction turn left (signposted Hedging) and continue along this lane, passing through the hamlet of Hedging and Primmore Farm on your left, until you reach a footpath sign in the hedge next to a gap into a field. Cross the field diagonally to the far corner, where you reach a gap between hedges and a field track.

4. Walk along the track into the next field, where you walk with the hedge on your left until you reach a gap in the hedge on your left. Go through the gap and turn right, heading towards houses and the canal to find a stile in the hedge to the right of a gate. Cross over the swing bridge and canal and turn left and onto the towpath. Continue along the towpath for some distance,

Swing Bridge

20

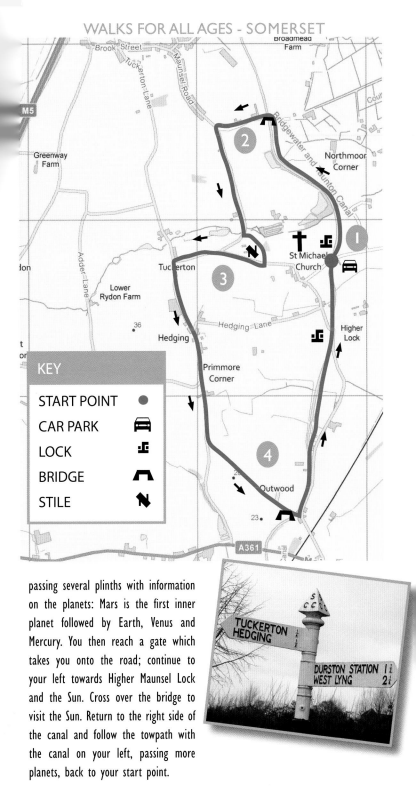

KEY

START POINT	●
CAR PARK	🚗
LOCK	🔒
BRIDGE	⌐⌐
STILE	↗

passing several plinths with information on the planets: Mars is the first inner planet followed by Earth, Venus and Mercury. You then reach a gate which takes you onto the road; continue to your left towards Higher Maunsel Lock and the Sun. Cross over the bridge to visit the Sun. Return to the right side of the canal and follow the towpath with the canal on your left, passing more planets, back to your start point.

GLASTONBURY TOR

A circular walk of 2½ miles (4km) which takes you to the top of Glastonbury Tor; with the steep climb it should take at least 1½ hours. The Tor is 518ft (158m) above sea level.

This circular walk takes you from the centre of the town of Glastonbury, climbing up the famous Tor, on a concrete path with steps in places, to St Michael's Church Tower and descending down by a concrete path with steps, then crossing through fields and back to the town centre.

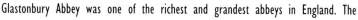
To the Tor

The mystic town of Glastonbury is situated on the Somerset Levels 23 miles (35km) from Bristol and is noted for its myths and legends as well as the famous Glastonbury Festival. The Festival site is actually situated a few miles from Glastonbury at a small village called Pilton.

Glastonbury Ruin

Glastonbury Abbey was one of the richest and grandest abbeys in England. The first part of the Abbey was built in the 7th century by the Saxon king Ine of Wessex. Then when the Normans invaded England and conquered the Saxons they took over the Abbey and added additional buildings, and the Abbey became the richest monastery in England. It is said that King Arthur and Queen Guinevere are buried at the Abbey. Many successive abbots of the monastery lived in great splendour over the years, but during the time of Henry VIII and the dissolution of the monasteries Glastonbury Abbey and all its land and properties were sold off or leased to new lay occupiers.

Over the centuries many pilgrims have visited Glastonbury and one of those is reported to have been Joseph of Arimathea, the uncle of Jesus, who brought with him the Holy Grail, the cup that was used by Christ at the Last Supper. It is said that Joseph landed in Avalon at Wearyall Hill and stuck his staff into the ground. Overnight it took root and grew into what we know today as the famous Glastonbury Thorn.

THE NATIONAL TRUST
GLASTONBURY TOR
Please respect this special place
No Camping
No Fires

This thorn tree flowers at Christmas time and a sprig is cut each year and sent to the Queen. Joseph hid the Holy Grail for safe keeping and buried it below the Tor. A spring then emerged and the water which flows is said to give eternal youth. This is known as the Chalice Well and you will pass it on your walk to the Tor.

Glastonbury Tor is known as one of the most spiritual sites in the country. Its pagan significance is still celebrated today by Christian pilgrims visiting the Tor. Glastonbury Tor is managed by the National Trust and was at one time, many hundreds of years ago, an island as much of the Somerset Levels were under water. The medieval church of St Michael remained in place until 1275, when an earthquake was recorded in England that destroyed the church. The second church was built in the 14th century and remained on the hill until the dissolution of the monasteries in 1539, when the Tor became a place of execution.

Prayer Wheels

THE BASICS

Distance in miles and km: 2½ miles (4km)

Gradient: Steep climb to top of Tor

Severity: Easy with Steep climb

Approx min time to walk: 1½ hours or longer with steep climb

Stiles: No stiles

Maps: OS Explorer 141 Cheddar Gorge and Mendip Hills West

Path description: Pavements, concrete track up Tor, steps, field paths

Start Point: Public car park at Abbey Car Park GR 499 388

Parking: Public car park at Abbey Car Park GR 499 388

Dog friendly: On leads

Public Toilets: Abbey Car Park and in the Town

Nearest food: Various restaurants and cafes in town

GLASTONBURY TOR WALK

1. Leave the car park, turn left and walk ahead along the pavement up Fishers Hill and passing the Catholic Church on your right. Follow the pavement around to the left, passing Somerset Rural Life Museum on your right, until you reach a roundabout. Taking care, cross over the road and turn right: you are now on Chilkwell Street. Continue ahead, passing old cottages on your left and the Rifleman Pub on your right, and you will soon reach the Chalice Well and Gardens on your left. A short distance after the Chalice Well you meet a road, Wellhouse Lane. Here you turn left and almost immediately right again.

2. Continue ahead to reach a kissing gate and the entrance to the National Trust's Glastonbury Tor. Follow the zig-zag footpath up the steep hill to the top of the Tor and St Michael's Tower. From the top of the hill the views are spectacular across the Somerset Levels and beyond. After spending some time at the top of the Tor you can descend by the shorter concrete footpath which starts on the right-hand side of St Michael's Tower and continues down to two kissing gates and the road.

3. On reaching the road turn left and continue ahead along the road, ignoring the road to the right, until you reach a kissing gate in the hedge on your right signpost Dod Lane. Go through the gate and across a field to a further kissing gate and continue ahead along a path between two hedges to reach a road. Do not follow it left but go straight ahead.

4. Pass through a metal kissing gate with views over the town of Glastonbury. Follow a grassy path down to another kissing gate. You are now heading back towards the town. After going through the gate and onto the road, note the Tibetan Prayer Wheels on your left. The prayer wheels are full of thousands of prayers and turning the wheels in a clockwise direction sends the prayers out into the world.

5. Continue ahead down the road to meet the main road. Turn right and then cross the road and turn right and then

Abbey Barn

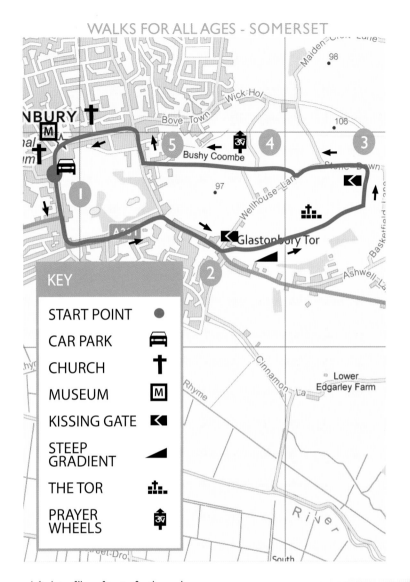

KEY

START POINT	●
CAR PARK	🚗
CHURCH	†
MUSEUM	M
KISSING GATE	◤
STEEP GRADIENT	◢
THE TOR	⛪
PRAYER WHEELS	🕉

left into Silver Street. Continue along this road, passing a car park on your left and following the road as it curves around to right; you then enter the High Street opposite the parish church of St John's. To return to the start point of the walk turn left on reaching the High Street and walk beside the shops following the pavement around to the left, passing the Town Hall on your left and then back to the car park

Town Centre

AXBRIDGE

Two circular walks of 4 miles (6.5km) or 1½ miles (2.5km) around the village of Axbridge and Cheddar Reservoir. This interesting and pleasant walk takes you around the Medieval Town of Axbridge and onto the banks of Cheddar Reservoir.

It is mostly on pavements and hard track around the reservoir with a short distance across fields and along a drove which can be muddy in wet weather. Parking is in Axbridge off Moorland Street. Axbridge is found off the A371 to Weston-super-Mare.

Axbridge Square

Axbridge is situated in the Sedgemoor district of Somerset on the River Axe, near the southern edge of the Mendip Hills. This ancient medieval town dates back to the 10th century and was certainly inhabited by the Romans, who used to mine the lead which was found in the nearby Mendip Hills.

Axbridge grew in the Tudor period as a centre for cloth manufacture. This was reflected in its early royal charters allowing it to hold markets and fairs and to become a royal borough. It even had its own mint, with coins showing the town's symbol on them, the "Lamb and Flag".

King John's Hunting Lodge is a 15th-century wood-framed jettied building and stands majestically in the market place. Today it is owned by the National Trust and is rented to the Axbridge District Museum Trust. The Museum is well worth a visit and houses a collection illustrating local history and the geology and archaeology of the area.

Horn's Lane Path

Cheddar Reservoir is an artificial reservoir owned by Bristol Water. The reservoir is supplied with water taken from the Cheddar Yeo river in Cheddar Gorge. The Reservoir lies to the west of the village of Cheddar and south-east of the town of Axbridge. It is roughly circular in shape, is surrounded by large earth banks and is designated as a Site of Special Scientific Interest due to its wintering waterfowl populations. The path around the lake is not a public footpath but Bristol Water has given permission for the public to walk around the lake.

Cheddar Gorge and the village of Cheddar are located some 3 miles (5km) from Axbridge. The famous Cheddar Gorge and Caves are located on the northern edge of Cheddar village. It is the largest gorge in the United Kingdom and includes several show caves including Gough's Cave. It is also the site of several limestone quarries. The village gave its name to Cheddar cheese and has also been a centre for strawberry growing.

Axbridge Church

THE BASICS

Distance in miles and km: 4miles (6.5km) or 1½ miles (2.5km)

Gradient: Flat walking

Severity: Easy flat walking

Approx min time to walk: 2 hours or 40 mins

Stiles: Two stiles

Maps: OS Explorer 141 Cheddar Gorge, Mendip Hills West

Path description: Pavements, hard surfaces, open fields

Start Point: Moorland Street car park GR 430 545

Parking: Moorland Street off Market Square GR 430 545

Dog friendly: On leads

Public Toilets: At parking area

Nearest food: Axbridge Town

AXBRIDGE WALK

1. Start in the town square, where you can see the half-timbered King John's Hunting Lodge. Walk up the High Street between the Hunting Lodge and the Lamb Inn, noticing the medieval houses, the Drugstore Gallery and others, until you meet Horn Lane. Turn right into Horn Lane and follow the narrow lane uphill and around to the right, continuing along this lane between high stone walls to reach the church of St John the Baptist.

3. Walk down the lane; there is a blue sign for the yacht club at the beginning of the lane on your right. You then reach the Reservoir gates.*** Here you have a choice to lengthen the walk by walking around the Reservoir with wonderful views of the Mendips or taking the shorter option directly back to Axbridge.

2. On reaching the church do not go down the steps back into the square but turn left in front of the church steps and after a short distance turn right into Church Lane. On reaching the road cross the road with care and turn left and continue ahead along Cheddar Road, ignoring any side roads to the left and right. You pass a bus shelter/stop on your left and the Reservoir Motel on your right. Continue until you see a signpost on your left directing you to the Reservoir.

4. After the walk around the Reservoir you return back to the Reservoir gates.*** You then follow the track that branches off to the right on the bend of the lane. The long and the short walk follow this track through the wooded copse with fields on your right, to reach a gate and a stile. Cross over the stile and continue ahead along the narrow field, keeping slightly to your right, with the hedge on your right, to go though a gateway gap between two trees and over a small bridge. Follow around to your right to find a further stile ahead, passing an old building on your left. Climb over

Mendip Hills

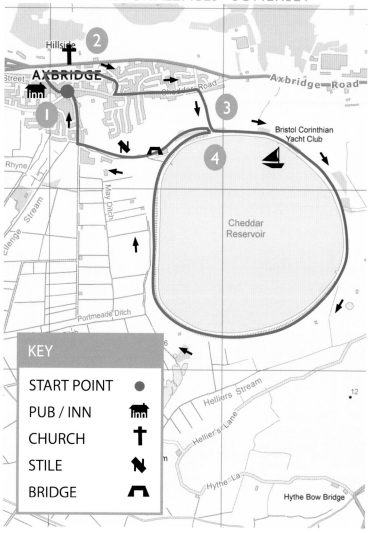

KEY

START POINT	●
PUB / INN	🏠
CHURCH	†
STILE	Ⰶ
BRIDGE	⌂

the stile and bear right to follow an old drove back to Axbridge, passing Moorland Farm Shop to reach the end of the drove. Turn right and follow the road ahead through houses. You are now in Moorland Street, continuing on until you reach your starting point and car park.

BREAN DOWN HEADLAND

A Circular walk of 3½ miles (5.5km) over headland with wonderful views. This interesting walk around the Brean Down headland takes you to the top of the ridge from sea level via steps which zig-zag steeply to the top.

This open and exposed headland is owned by the National Trust and it offers wonderful views of the Bristol Channel together with the two islands of Steep Holm and Flat Holm and the Welsh Coast.

Brean Down

Once you have climbed the steep steps to the ridge of the headland the walking is easy along a grass track towards the end of the peninsula, where you will find a 19th-century fortification built to defend the upper limits of the Bristol Channel against an invasion from the French. You are able to visit the fort, which has a

number of information boards, and explore the old gun defences. The return route is along a rough road passing a number of fortifications built during the two world wars, with wonderful views of the Channel and the bay of Weston-super-Mare.

The village of Brean lies on the shores of the Somerset coast and runs alongside the beach. Brean Down is one of the most dramatic landmarks of the Somerset coastline, and offers an opportunity for lovely walks. In Brean village and along the coast there are a number of holiday and leisure parks.

Brean Down is a massive, high finger of limestone escarpment which juts into the Bristol Channel and is the continuation of the Mendip Hills. Steep Holm and Flat Holm, which can be seen out in the Channel, are the true end of the Mendip Hills. The Down stands 320 feet (97m) high and the views from the top are truly spectacular, looking out over the Bristol Channel towards South Wales and over the Somerset Levels and stunning coastline.

The fort at the end of the peninsula was built in the 1860s as part of a grand scheme of defences devised to see off the threat of a French invasion. Such

Barracks

fortifications have since become known as Palmerston's Follies on account of the fact that they became obsolete within just a few years of being built as a result of large-scale improvements in naval gunnery. The Fort was home to three 7-inch rifled muzzle-loading guns. Working with similar batteries on the Welsh coast and on the islands of Steep Holm and Flat Holm the fort served to protect the city of Bristol from raiders navigating up the Severn Estuary. The fort was destroyed in 1900 by a rogue artilleryman who discharged his weapon down the ventilation shaft. The site was rendered unusable and remained out of use until World War II. It is rich in wildlife, history and archaeology and is a Site of Special Scientific Interest.

THE BASICS

Distance in miles and km: 3½ miles (5.5km)

Gradient: Steep climb initially

Severity: Easy walking

Approx min time to walk: 1 hour 40 minutes + time to view fort

Stiles: No stiles

Maps: OS Explorer 153 Weston-super-Mare

Path description: Grassy track and rough road

Start Point: National Trust Car Park GR 296 585

Parking: National Trust Car Park or Beach Car Park GR 296 585

Dog friendly: On leads

Public Toilets: None available on route

Nearest food: Bird Garden Cafe

BREAN DOWN HEADLAND

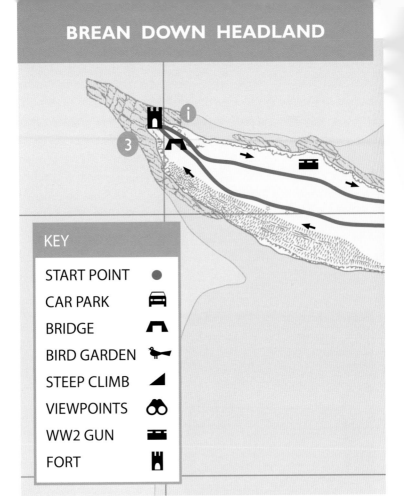

KEY

START POINT	●
CAR PARK	🚗
BRIDGE	⌂
BIRD GARDEN	🐦
STEEP CLIMB	◢
VIEWPOINTS	👓
WW2 GUN	▄▄
FORT	♜

1. You start this interesting walk by leaving the National Trust car park, in the village of Brean, to your right and walking along the stony road towards the Bird Gardens. Keeping to the left of the café, follow the track towards the steps and the headland which can be seen ahead of you. You then climb the steep steps to the top of the limestone escarpment. It is a steep climb, so stop and take in the panoramic views of the Somerset Levels and the Bristol Channel and, on a good day, the Welsh coast.

2. At the top of the headland turn left and head westward along the grassy worn path

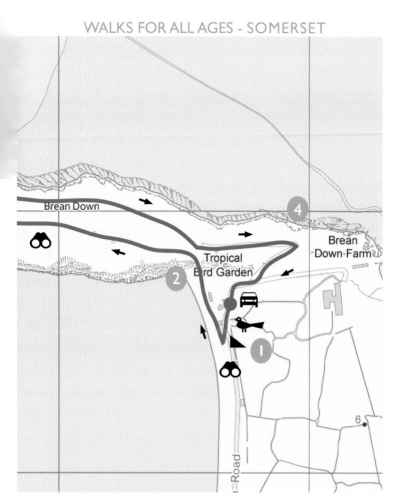

climbing gently to the highest point of the Down. En route you will pass the remains of both an old Roman temple and ancient field systems. You then reach a trig point, where you should stop and take time out to admire the wonderful view of Flat Holm and Steep Holm ahead of you and south to Hinkley Point nuclear power station and beyond to Exmoor.

3. Continue to the end of the peninsula, where you will find extensive fortifications built about 1870. Entry to the old fortifications is free and there are a number of information boards. You visit the site by crossing a small bridge to the right of the buildings.

4. After visiting the fort you return by crossing the small bridge and keeping slightly left and head along the old tarmac road which used to bring men and munitions to the fort. Continue to follow the old road, passing Second World War gun emplacements and with wonderful views of Weston-super-Mare and the River Axe estuary on your left. The track then bears around to your right and descends gently down to a gate. Go through the gate and, keeping right, follow the track back to the car park.

CLEVEDON POET'S WALK

A 2½-mile (4km) circular seaside walk with wonderful views across the Bristol Channel. This beautiful scenic walk from the seafront promenade at Clevedon is along tarmac paths which take you around the cliff-top headland.

You join the Poet's Walk and retrace your steps back to Clevedon Pier. It is a walk suitable for all the family, but there are a few steps to climb and one or two gentle hills. Parking on the seafront or Salthouse Fields. Clevedon can be reached from Junction 20 of the M5.

Walk Start

Clevedon is a sedate Victorian seaside resort that sits proudly above the Bristol Channel and has plenty to offer all ages. Sand gives way to a pebbled shoreline with wonderful views of the Bristol Channel and the Welsh Coast.

This resort became very popular in Victorian times due to the short branch line from the main railway at Yatton. Another railway also served the town: the Weston, Clevedon and Portishead Light Railway, which opened in 1897 and closed in 1940. Much of the Victorian architecture in the town is unspoilt.

Memorial

Clevedon Pier was opened in 1869, and is one of the earliest examples of a Victorian pier still in existence in the United Kingdom. It was constructed of iron rails originally intended for use on Brunel's South Wales Railway.

The seafront includes ornamental gardens, a Victorian bandstand, and other visitor attractions. The Salthouse Field has a light railway running round the perimeter and there are donkey rides during the summer. The shore is a mixture of pebbled beaches and low rocky cliffs, with the old harbour being at the western edge of the

Poet's Path

town at the mouth of the River Yeo. Clevedon's coastal walks offer stunning views of the coastline and Welsh mountains which have inspired many great writers including Tennyson, Thackeray and Coleridge. Coleridge used to live in Clevedon in a cottage on Old Church Road.

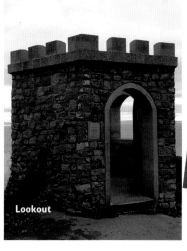

Lookout

THE BASICS

Distance in miles and km: 2½ miles (4km)

Gradient: One small climb

Severity: Easy walking

Approx min time to walk: 2 hours

Stiles: No stiles

Maps: OS Explorer 153 Weston-super-Mare

Path description: Footpaths and wooded track

Start Point: Sea front at Clevedon GR 402 719

Parking: Sea front at Clevedon GR 402 719

Dog friendly: On leads

Public Toilets: Sea front

Nearest food: A selection of cafes and restaurants along sea front

CLEVEDON POET'S WALK

1. You start the walk at Clevedon Pier. Leaving the pier behind you, walk along the Promenade towards Clevedon Sailing Club. Note the wonderful views across the Bristol Channel to the Welsh coast. In the channel you can see the islands of Steep Holm and Flat Holm, which are actually part of the Mendip Hills and are now both nature reserves. Pass in front of the sailing club and continue on the Promenade, passing the bandstand which was built in 1883, and the water fountain on your left. Continue ahead following the Promenade, passing the Little Harp Inn on your left. Head toward the Salthouse Inn, passing the boating lake on your right.

Clevedon Pier

2. To the right of the Salthouse Inn you will see a flight of stone steps leading into the woods. Climb these steps and turn right at the top and follow the path ahead until you meet a large stone seat. Turn to your left and follow the track up to the lookout tower which was erected by Eric Ferdinand Beeston, and was said to been used by the Finzel Family, Sugar Importers, to view the sugar ships coming from the West Indies into Bristol.

3. Continue to follow the path uphill until you reach a fingerpost, and bear to the left in the direction of St Andrew's Church. As you walk along this path you look down onto St Andrew's Church and the churchyard set in this beautiful location on the headland. Follow the path until you meet another path coming in from the left. You bear right and continue to the road and the lychgate to the church. Keeping right, follow the road between St Andrew's Centre car park and the cemetery on your right. You then reach a busier road; here you turn right and walk along a footpath to a wooden barrier and old boat yard.

4. You will see ahead of you a fingerpost showing you the direction of the Poet's Walk. Turn right and follow the path

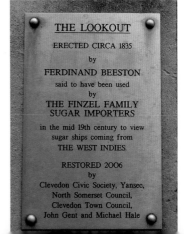

THE LOOKOUT

ERECTED CIRCA 1835
by
FERDINAND BEESTON
said to have been used
by
THE FINZEL FAMILY
SUGAR IMPORTERS

in the mid 19th century to view
sugar ships coming from
THE WEST INDIES.

RESTORED 2006
by
Clevedon Civic Society, Yansec,
North Somerset Council,
Clevedon Town Council,
John Gent and Michael Hale

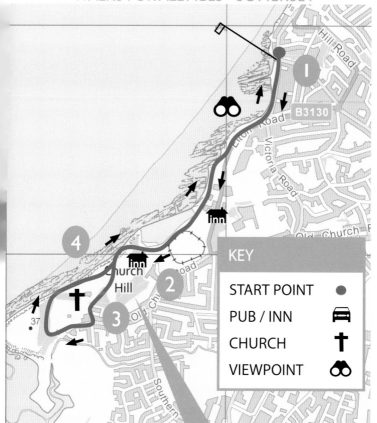

KEY

START POINT	●
PUB / INN	🚘
CHURCH	✝
VIEWPOINT	👓

uphill to the top of the headland. Stop and take time to look at the views. All along this path there are a number of seats for you to rest and enjoy the view. Continue along the path, which takes you around the headland and passes St Andrew's Church and churchyard from the other side. This path then meets up at the fingerpost where you turned left to St Andrew's Church. Continue ahead along the previous path you walked, passing the lookout and down to the stone seat. Turn right back to the top of the steps you ascended and retrace your steps along the promenade and back to the pier.

BATH

A 4-mile (6.5km) circular walk around the beautiful city of Bath. This interesting walk takes you from the centre of Bath through the Georgian streets, along the Kennet and Avon Canal and the River Avon.

It visits the Botanical Gardens and passes the well-known Royal Crescent, the Circus, the Pump Room and the Roman Baths. If you would also like a little retail therapy the walk takes you through the main shopping area and its many arcades. The walk is mostly on surfaced paths and the canal towpath. There are several car parks within the city and three Park & Rides at Lansdown, Newbridge and Odd Down.

Bath Abbey

The city of Bath was inscribed as a World Heritage Site in 1987 and is a major centre for tourism. Founded by the Romans as a thermal spa, Bath also became an important centre of the wool industry in the Middle Ages. Bath has over 5,000 listed buildings and a large part of the city is a conservation area. The beautiful Georgian buildings built out of locally quarried Bath Stone remind us that the city was once and still is today a very important spa and cultural centre.

Bath has a number of public parks, the largest being the Royal Victoria Park. This park is overlooked by the spectacular Royal Crescent, one of the many Georgian terraces which can be found in the city.

Bath is located on the River Avon and connected to Bristol and the sea by this river. The Kennet and Avon Canal was built in 1810 to join the Avon to the River Thames and

Royal Crescent

London. The Canal was closed for many years but has been restored and is now used for boating, walking and cycling and is also important for wildlife conservation.

BATH WALK.

1. This walk starts in the centre of the beautiful city of Bath outside Bath Abbey. Facing Bath Abbey with the Pump Room on your right and keeping to the right of the Abbey make your way across the square to the corner of York Street. The Tourist Information Centre is on your left as you enter York Street. Walk along York Street to the road and the river. Here you cross the road and then go left following the stone wall around to your right to reach Pulteney Bridge. Looking over the wall you will get a wonderful view of Pulteney Weir and the River Avon.

Assembly Rooms

Distance in miles and km: 4 miles (6.5km)

Gradient: Small inclines

Severity: Easy walking

Approx min time to walk: 2 hours

Stiles: No stiles

Maps: OS Explorer 155 Bristol Bath

Path description: Surfaced paths , canal towpaths, gravel path

Start Point: Bath Abbey GR 750 647

Parking: Southgate Car Park or Park & Ride

Dog friendly: On leads

Public Toilets: Several in the town

Nearest food: Bath city

THE BASICS

BATH WALK CONT.

2. Turn right onto Pulteney Bridge and walk over the bridge with shops on either side and continue ahead towards the Holburne Museum, which you can see at the end of a wonderful row of Georgian terraced houses. On reaching Holburne Museum, cross over the road to the museum and go left, passing the Museum entrance on your right, and on the corner turn right into a small but attractive park, Sydney Gardens.

3. Continue ahead along a tarmac path through the gardens, crossing over two bridges, firstly the railway and secondly the canal. Bearing slightly right, follow the path alongside the tennis courts and around to the right to reach the park entrance and road. Cross the road and go right, ignoring the road to your left ("Sham Castle Lane"), but take the adjacent track with waymarks on the pillars to the canal.

4. Keeping to your left, follow the canal towpath until you reach a road. Cross the road and go right, and at the end of the wall and next to Tesco Express turn sharp left and down some steps to reach the canal again. Turn right and continue to follow the canal towpath, passing several locks to reach a further road and on to meet another road. Here you go left along a walkway over the lock and left down the steps to meet the canal. The canal is now on your right and you follow the path until you reach the end of the canal and the meeting point with the River Avon. Cross over the narrow road and follow the

walkway beside the river, walking under two metal girder bridges until you meet a pedestrian footbridge. Cross and turn left and cross a dual carriageway and continue to walk along the footpath with the river on your left until you find a track on your left leading down to the river and the cycle/footpath.

Bath Residence

5. Continue to follow the footpath under several bridges. The first bridge is the girder Midland Bridge and then the covered bridge which leads to Sainsbury's, and then continue under a further suspension bridge. After the suspension bridge continue ahead and just before a further girder bridge take the narrow pathway to your right which takes you onto Midland Road. Turn right and ahead you can see Victoria Park. Walk to the busy road and cross the road, going to your left, and continue to the corner of Park Lane. Turn right and walk up the hill and then turn right through a gap in the wall into the open park. Cross the road and go left and ahead you will see the metal gates into the Botanic Gardens.

6. Enter the Botanic Gardens, go right and follow the many paths to a pond. Pass around the pond and near the Minerva Temple exit the gardens through metal gates and onto the road. Opposite

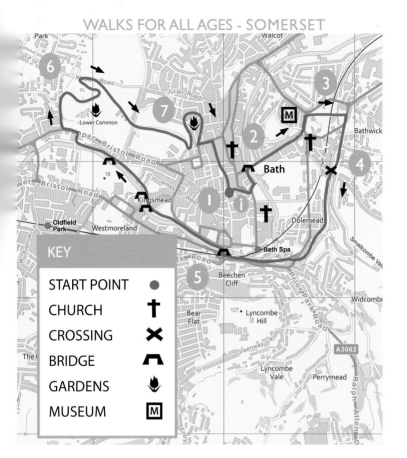

is another Garden known as the Dell. Cross the road and go right and follow path a short distance. Across the road to your right you will see a fingerpost and a gravel track which goes diagonally across the open park. Take this gravel path until you reach a road and opposite a lane which is marked as 'no entry'. Follow the lane, passing old glasshouses on your right, until you reach a road. Cross the road ("Marlborough Buildings") and follow the tarmac path through bollards, which takes you across the park in front of the well-known Royal Crescent. On reaching a fingerpost on your right turn left towards the Royal Crescent and at the road junction turn right and follow the road into the Circus.

7. Keeping to the left side of the Circus take the first exit on the left into Bennett Street. Walk a short distance along and turn right, passing the Assembly Rooms and Costume Museum on your left, and continue down the narrow street. On reaching a T-junction turn right and follow the street around to your left before meeting metal hand rails and the busy George Street. Go left and cross the road to enter Milsom Street on your right. Continue ahead down through the shopping area, passing along Milsom Street, Burton Street, Union Street and Stall Street. The Abbey Churchyard is on your left through pillars.

FRESHFORD

A circular 6-mile (9.5km) countryside walk. This walk takes you from the quiet village of Freshford in the beautiful Avon Valley to Avoncliff, a small hamlet located next to the River Avon and the towpath of the Kennet and Avon Canal.

Avoncliffe

The paths take you across pastureland through villages and along the river bank. The paths are undulating and can be muddy in wet weather. Park in the village of Freshford, which is located 6 miles (10km) south-east of Bath off the A36.

Freshford is some 6 miles (10km) from Bath and 3 miles (5km) west of Bradford on Avon and lies on the extreme southern boundary of the Cotswolds, in an area that has only recently been included in the AONB (Area of Outstanding Natural

Bungalow Path

Beauty). The beautiful village sits above the convergence of the rivers Frome and Avon. The walk features all that is best about this area with the rivers, valleys and green rolling hills forming an exceptional backdrop for attractive stone villages, historic churches and country houses, including manors at both Westwood and Iford.

In the small village of Iford, Iford Manor is located. The Manor is best known for its Grade I internationally listed gardens, designed during the early part of the 20th century by the garden architect Harold Peto. The gardens are open to the public on certain days.

The walk also takes you on to the village of Westwood. Here you will find the magnificent church of St Mary the Virgin, dating back to the 13th century. Next to the church is Westwood Manor. This small manor house was built over three centuries and was once owned by a wealthy clothier in medieval times but is now managed by the National Trust.

Iford Manor

Avoncliff is where the Kennet and Avon Canal crosses the River Avon and the railway via the Avoncliff Aqueduct, which was built by John Rennie between 1797 and 1801.

As you stand on the Aqueduct you will see a most beautiful weir on the River Avon by the side of the 16th-century Cross Guns Inn. A beautiful scene in the summer. The River Avon rises just north of the village of Acton Turville in South Gloucestershire, before flowing through Wiltshire. In its lower reaches from Bath to the Severn Estuary at Avonmouth near Bristol and out into the Bristol Channel the river is also navigable and is known as the "Avon Navigation".

Kissing Gate

Mill Cottages

THE BASICS

Distance in miles and km: 6 miles (9.5km)

Gradient: Undulating

Severity: Easy walking

Approx min time to walk: 3 hours

Stiles: 4 stiles

Maps: OS Explorer 155 and 156

Path description: Field paths, canal path and tracks, can be muddy

Start Point: Freshford Inn GR 790 600

Parking: Park in village

Dog friendly: On leads

Public Toilets: None on route

Nearest food: Avoncliffe cafe and Inn, Inn at Freshford, Inn at Westwood

FRESHFORD WALK

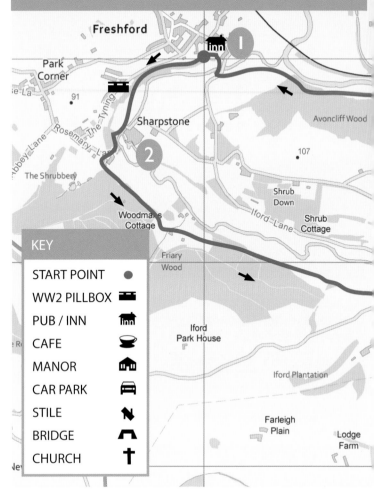

KEY

START POINT	●
WW2 PILLBOX	▬
PUB / INN	🏠
CAFE	☕
MANOR	🏛
CAR PARK	🚗
STILE	ᛗ
BRIDGE	∏
CHURCH	†

1. This walk starts at The Inn, Freshford. With your back to the inn, turn right and in a few yards turn right again through a gate to follow a footpath sign. In 50 yards (50m), keep on the path as it bears right uphill into woodland. Pass through a gate at the top of the climb, turn left and continue following the downhill path above the River Frome to a gate by the river. Cross the field ahead to the next gate before going over a field, passing an old pillbox, to a gate and quiet lane.

2. Turn right and, in 150 yards (150m), follow a bridleway on the left by Dunkirk Mill Cottage around to the frontage of Middle House. Turn left and follow an enclosed track across the valley side for 500 yards (500m), to a hand gate on the edge of Friary. Drop downhill across an open area of grassland to join the lane in this rural hamlet. Turn left and, in 20 yards, right along a path across open grassland, opposite a property called Whistlers Hollow, to a gateway and field. Cross this field to reach a kissing gate at

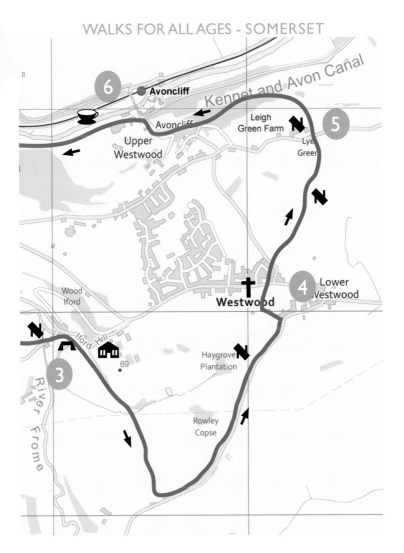

the entrance to Friary wood and follow the main woodland path through to a stile and large riverside meadow.

3. Walk the length of this large field to a stile in the far right corner, join a road and turn left into Iford, crossing the River Frome to reach a junction in front of Iford Manor. Turn right uphill and, in 120 yards (120m), fork right along a bridleway. Follow this enclosed track for half a mile (1km) through to the Farleigh Hungerford to Westwood road.

4. Turn left and in 500 yards (500m), ignoring the first fingerpost on the right, cross the second stile on the right to join a waymarked footpath. Follow the path through a small copse, before following the left edges of two fields to a gate opposite Westwood Manor and church. Enter the churchyard following the path to the right around the church and then follow a lane on the left by the door. Continue ahead as it bears around to the right to meet a road. Cross the road and continue along the road opposite to a stile on the left-

hand bend, with a sign for Limes Farm Cottage on a wall.

5. Cross the stile and follow a footpath across the right edges of three fields to a stone stile in the right corner of the third field. Cross over the stile, turn left and walk diagonally across the field to a wooden and stone stile which brings you out onto a road at Lye Cross.

6. Cross the road and go through the garden gate of bungalow No 102 opposite, with a footpath arrow on the gate. Go just to the right of the bungalow and down to the bottom of the garden through a half barrier and on down a path to a stone stile. Cross over the stile and continue straight down and across to another stile. Ahead is the Avon Valley with the market town of Bradford on Avon to your right. Continue down left to a stile and continue left over the field bank which takes you to a stile into the bottom field. You then follow the left field edge, which is directly above the Kennet and Avon Canal, to find a small iron gate at the entrance to woodland.

7. Follow the main path through the woodland to a lane, and follow the lane to the right downhill to the canal and hamlet of Avoncliff. Immediately past Lily's Cafe, turn left along a track that passes a former poorhouse that now has been converted into apartments. Just past this building, pass through a gate ahead and follow an enclosed path running between the river and woodland to a kissing gate and large open field. Follow the riverside field to a kissing gate and in next field keep the river on your right and walk to a kissing gate to join a road, and then turn right to return to The Inn at Freshford.

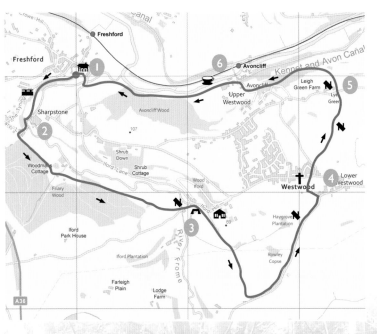

STANTON DREW STONES

A circular walk of 3¼ miles (5km). This easy walk starts at the Stanton Drew Stone Circle and takes you beside the River Chew, along the beautiful valley towards the village of Pensford.

Before reaching Pensford village you will see a magnificent viaduct and you will then return from Pensford back along the river to Stanton Drew. Parking is at 'The Cove' car park in Stanton Drew village which is located 6 miles (10km) south of Bristol off the A368.

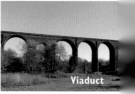

Viaduct

Stanton Drew is very much a country village, located 6 miles (10km) south of Bristol with active farming and a traditional community. The village is most

famous for its prehistoric Stanton Drew stone circles, the largest being the Great Circle, a henge monument consisting of the second largest stone circle in Britain (after Avebury).

The stone circle is 370 feet (113m) in diameter and probably consisted of 30 stones, of which 27 survive today. Also within the village, in the garden of the village pub, is another group of three large stones called The Cove, which was once part of the larger stone circle. The Stanton Drew stone circles are in the care of English Heritage but lie on private land, accessible on payment of a £1.00 entrance fee to be dropped into an honesty box.

The village of Pensford is a ribbon village lying alongside the A37 road. It was identified as being of special architectural and historic interest and was designated as a Conservation Area in May 1988. The name Pensford is believed to mean "The animal pens by the ford". During the 14th to 16th centuries Pensford was a cloth centre based on local wool and during the 19th and 20th

Chew Valley

centuries the main industry was coal mining, with Pensford and the surrounding area forming a major part of the Somerset coalfield. The magnificent railway viaduct, which is built of local stone and can be seen on the walk, opened in 1873 to carry the Bristol and North Somerset Railway over the valley of the River Chew. The Pensford Viaduct is no longer used as a railway line and since 1984 has been Grade II listed. St Thomas à Becket Church dates from the 14th century, although only the tower remains from that date.

The River Chew rises at Chewton Mendip and flows for 17 miles (27km) before joining the River Avon at Keynsham and forms the beautiful Chew Valley. The River Chew has been dammed at Litton and Chew Stoke to form three reservoirs, providing drinking water to the Bristol Water region. The largest of these is Chew Valley Lake, known worldwide for fly fishing and one of the most important sites in the country for wintering wildfowl.

Stone Circle

THE BASICS

Distance in miles and km: 3¼ miles (5km)

Gradient: One short slope

Severity: Easy walking

Approx min time to walk: 1¼ hours

Stiles: No stiles

Maps: OS Explorer 155 Bristol and Bath

Path description: Field paths, can be muddy

Start Point: Stanton Drew Stone Circle GR 597 632

Parking: The Cove (Druids Arms) GR 597 631

Dog friendly: On leads

Public Toilets: None on route

Nearest food: Inns at Stanton Drew and Pensford

1. With your back to the car park turn to your right and walk, passing the Druids Arms, and take the first turning on your right, following this road round right to reach a kissing gate and sign to Stone Circles. Through the gate bear right to join a tarmac track heading towards farm buildings. Follow this track, going through several gates, before reaching a sewage works. Go through a gate to the right of the sewage works and continue across the field to reaching a kissing gate in the hedge.

2. Follow the field path along the edge of the field with the hedge on your left and then bear right at the second telegraph pole to a gate and road. Cross the road and take a short track up to a gate and then follow the field path along the edge of the field to a further metal gate and road. Cross the road and go through a kissing gate next to a footpath fingerpost and continue ahead across a field to a further gate. Go through this gate and head down towards the river and follow the river bank to the lower gate next to the river and on towards the weir and mill buildings in distance. On reaching the weir go through

a wooden kissing gate onto a wide track and continue ahead passing Byemill, a former iron and copper battery mill that was in use from the 1600s until 1860.

3. Through the next kissing gate follow the path across the field with the river on left to find on your right a kissing gate, leading to a slight uphill path and wooden steps to enter open ground. Ahead you can see the magnificent arched viaduct. Continue to follow the path towards the viaduct over a small bridge and under the arched viaduct.

4. As you pass under the viaduct take the path to the left which takes you to a very old bridge and weir and towards the parish church at Pensford. Cross the bridge and keep left you enter an area with a garage workshop. Follow around to your right between buildings to reach a T-junction. The street sign "Mill Corner" is above you in the wall on your left and to your right on the pub wall there is a marking showing the flood level in 1968. Turn left and immediately left again following a footpath sign uphill back towards the viaduct and passing Viaduct House on your right.

5. On the brow of the hill you reach a gate and enter Culvery Woods and follow the wide, wooded track ahead down towards a kissing gate. Go through the gate and follow the path with the river on your left-hand side. The path takes you on to a gate near the side of the

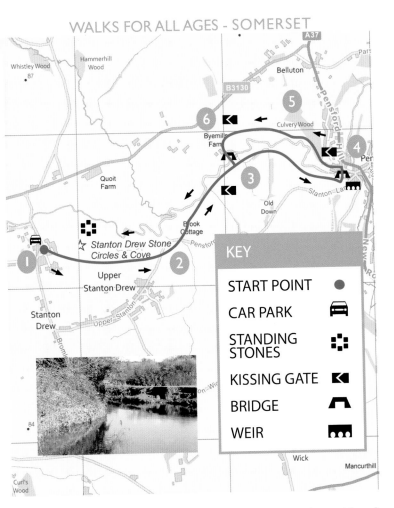

KEY

START POINT	●
CAR PARK	🚗
STANDING STONES	⬛
KISSING GATE	◤
BRIDGE	⌒
WEIR	⬛

river. Go through this gate and continue ahead across a field to a gate that can be seen in the hedge. Go through the gate and over a small bridge and through another gate and then across the field and up to the lower kissing gate in the corner of the hedges. Go through this gate and across a field to a further gate and on to a further gate. Enter a small field and walk towards the houses, gate and road.

7. On reaching the road turn left and continue ahead between houses and back to Bye Mills weir. Cross over the bridge and weir and turn right through a kissing gate. You now retrace your steps back to the start point, keeping the river now on your right and going back on the same route as your outward journey.

CHEW VALLEY LAKE

Two circular nature walks of 2½ miles (4km) and 2 miles (3.2km). These two nature trail walks start at Woodford Lodge Woods, and take you along a path next to the lake, with wonderful views across the lake to the Mendip Hills and the surrounding area.

There are many seats along the route so that you can sit and enjoy the beautiful view and watch the wildfowl.

Lakeside

The Bittern Trail is reached from the Grebe Trail by the footbridge over a hollow brook. It is not a surfaced path and can be wet and muddy in wet weather. This trail runs along the East Shore, visits a bird hide and returns to the footbridge, then rejoins the Grebe Trail before retracing your steps back to the starting point, making a total circuit of 2½ miles (4km).

Chew Valley Lake can be found off the A368 road from Bristol. Parking is available at Woodford Lodge car park.

Chew Valley Lake is located on the northern edge of the Mendip Hills and is surrounded by meadows and woods. It is close to the villages of Chew Stoke, Chew Magna and Bishop Sutton.

Boardwalk

The lake is Bristol Water's biggest lake, with a perimeter of some 10 miles (16km) and a total capacity of 20,000 million litres. It is the fifth largest artificial lake in the United Kingdom. Construction of the lake started in November 1950 and took just over five years to complete. Sixteen farmhouses, eleven other houses and 2,000 acres of land were bought up and drowned by the rising waters, and three and a half miles (5½km) of road were diverted or widened.

The lake was built to provide water for Bristol. Water is pumped to the Barrow treatment works on the outskirts of Bristol, which supplies much of the southern part of the city.

Start Here

The lake also supplies water to other areas, including Shepton Mallet, via the nearby Stowey Treatment Works.

Working with the Avon Wildlife Trust, Somerset Wildlife Trust and other environmental groups, Bristol Water has encouraged various species of birds and plants, and has created a venue for visitors. Two short nature walks, the Grebe and Bittern trails, have been created at the Lake to allow the visitors to enjoy the scenery and watch for visiting wildfowl.

Iron bridge

Info Boards

THE BASICS

Distance in miles and km: 2½ miles (4km) or 2miles (3.2km)

Gradient: Flat walking

Severity: Easy walking

Approx min time to walk: 1 hour or 45 minutes

Stiles: No stiles

Maps: OS Explorer 141/155

Path description: Stony paths and wooded paths

Start Point: Woodford Lodge Woods GR 573 614

Parking: Woodford Lodge off Walley Lane GR 573 614

Dog friendly: Dogs allowed on Glebe Trail but not on the Bitterne Trail

Public Toilets: At parking area

Nearest food: Coffee shop. Children's play area next to café.

CHEW VALLEY LAKE WALK

1. The walk starts at the main car park by the side of the lake next to the cafe. Walk from the car park away from the cafe to the path signposted to your right. This path is off the drive as you enter into the car park. Follow the stony track with the lake on your right; there are many seats along this path for you to stop and watch the wild birds on the lake and admire the wonderful views of the lake and Denny Island, until it reaches a second car park. Continue through the car park to the information board ahead.

Lakeside Path

2. At the information board the path splits. Take the left-hand path, the Grebe Trail, which takes you into woodland. Continue along the path, which winds through the woods to open reed beds. Follow the path as it bends around to the right to meet a bridge on your left. If you wish to take a shorter route continue around to your right and follow the path back to the second car park and retrace your steps back to the start point.

3. To continue along the Bittern Trail, cross over the bridge and follow the path to the right and through the woods. You will then reach a wooden squeeze barrier; go through this barrier and cross a track between boulders. Turn right and follow the Bittern Trail along a stony path. Do not take the path through the woods but continue along the track to meet a small

bridge with metal rails. To your right is a track which takes you to a hide so that you can watch the wild birds in the reed beds and on the lake.

4. Continuing along the Bittern Trail, cross the small bridge and walk along the boardwalk through the trees until you meet a wide grassy track. Turn left and follow this wide track with fields on your right and woodland to the left to the point where you joined the signed Bittern Trail. Turn right through the barrier and retrace your steps through the woods and back across the bridge. Keeping to your

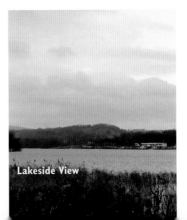
Lakeside View

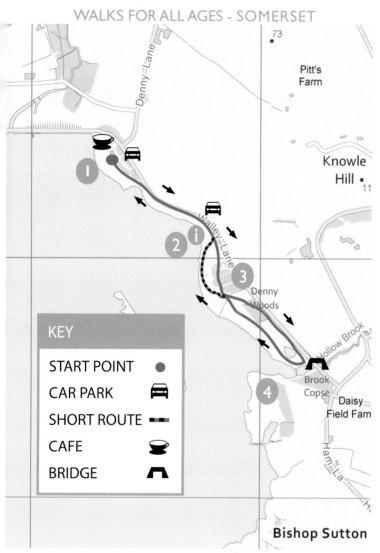

KEY

START POINT	●
CAR PARK	🚗
SHORT ROUTE	▬ ▬
CAFE	☕
BRIDGE	⌢

left, join the stony path and follow it along the side of the lake, which is now on your left. The path then meets a short, wider track on your left side. Here you can walk ahead on the wide grassy track or continue on the path through woods. Continue along the path to reach the information board and second car park. From the second car park retrace your steps back along the path to your start point at Woodford Lodge.

MELLS GREAT ELM

An easy 4-mile (6.5km) circular walk which starts in the village of Mells, near Frome. A fairly level walk which takes the walker from the interesting conservation village of Mells across fields and along the Colliers Way towards Great Elm.

At Great Elm you meet the Mells Stream and follow it along the river bank, passing the old Fussells iron works before returning to the village of Mells. Mells is located approximately 3 miles (5km) west of Frome off the A362. Park in the village near the Talbot Inn.

Great Elm Lane

Mells is the village where allegedly the English nursery rhyme "Little Jack Horner" was derived when Jack Horner was entrusted to take the deeds of Mells Manor to the King in London in 1543. The deeds were hidden in a pie and on the journey Jack took the deeds from the pie and on reaching London claimed he was the owner of Mells Manor.

Start Here

St Andrew's Church is notable not only for its beauty and its setting, but also for the number of famous people buried in the churchyard, and for the various works of art found there. If you take the path around to the right side of the church, in the second row of graves in the churchyard you will find the grave of Siegfried Sassoon, the poet and author, who was a regular visitor to Mells Manor.

The railway is now a Sustrans cycle and walking track known as the Colliers Way; it was the link between Radstock and Frome and has been closed for many years. It proved a useful means to transport coal from the now defunct Somerset coal mines. Just above the Conduit Bridge can be seen a long depression parallel with the railway line. This is the remains of the Dorset and Somerset Canal, which was started to transport coal, but was never finished.

Old Railway Bridge

Every year on Easter Monday the village of Mells holds a street fair known as "Mells Daffodil Day". There are many stalls and events taking place which make for a good day out for the family.

Mells Manor

Mells Church

THE BASICS

Distance in miles and km: 4miles (6.5kms)

Gradient: Small inclines.

Severity: Easy walking.

Approx min time to walk: 2½ hours.

Stiles: Three stiles.

Maps: OS Explorer 142 Shepton Mallet and Mendip Hills East.

Path description: Fields, old railway path and village roads.

Start Point: Talbot Inn GR 727 492.

Parking: Park in the village near the Talbot Inn.

Dog friendly: On leads.

Public Toilets: None on route.

Nearest food: Talbot Inn and village cafe.

Foxholes

1. Start the walk by taking the road next to the Talbot Inn which leads you to the church of St Andrew's, which is always open if you wish to visit it. Keeping to the left of the church you enter an avenue of yew trees and reach a field through the metal gate. Turn left to go over stile by the Mells Manor garden wall and immediately turn right uphill. Take the left-hand of the two clear paths over the brow (look back to see a full view of Mells Manor) to reach a stile

in the hedge, by an oak tree, leading to a further field.

2. Continue over the stile along the left-hand edge of the field to exit the field in the top left-hand corner, which leads you onto a road. Turn left and continue along the road until you reach a railway bridge. Just before the bridge turn left to join the Colliers Way and then immediately right in the direction of Frome to pass under

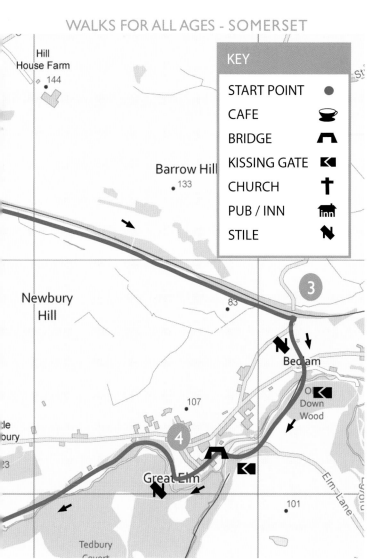

the Conduit Bridge. The Colliers Way is part of a national cycle network from Bath to Southampton. You continue along the Colliers Way, passing under Brick Kiln Farm Bridge, and along the route you will see various rocks with names of fruit trees. The trees have been planted to provide a linear orchard and hopefully enrichment for the traveller in the future. Continue along through two gates at Flowers Farm Bridge until you reach the end of the tarmac path and a road.

3. Turn right on the road away from the railway bridge and shortly take the first gate on the left. Go up into the field and over the brow and cross to find a stile in the far hedge leading to a road. Turn right and almost immediately take the first lane on the left, which drops down to the Mells Stream. Cross the stream by the bridge and turn right past the kissing gate onto

3 Cont.

a path that runs alongside the stream. Immediately on the right you will see the remains of an old mill in the stream. Pass between boulders and continue along, under the railway bridge and on, passing a beautiful converted mill house on the opposite bank. You then reach a kissing gate that comes out onto a road by the bridge at Great Elm.

4. Cross the road and pass through the kissing gate ahead and follow the track until you reach a gate leading to the railway line ahead. Turn right over the stile and the metal footbridge over the small stream. The path divides and you turn right and follow the path that goes across and picks up the main Mells Stream, bending left, so you are walking with the water on your right along the rugged Wadbury Valley until you reach a large footbridge on your right, which you cross and then turn left so that you are walking with the Mells Stream on your left. The whole valley is a green and secretive confusion of undergrowth hiding remains of the former Fussells of Mells iron edge tool works. Continue along this track, which eventually becomes tarmac, and you pass through a manicured lawn area with houses up on the hill on the right. Continue to follow the path ahead, which hugs the stream. (Do not go up the drive.) Before long you come to old high walls on your left and the first signs of the main iron works with glimpses through the crumbling walls of what was once one of the largest industrial sites in Europe. James Fussell originally started forging edge tools here in 1744 and demand increased from Europe and America to such an extent that nine water wheels were needed to drive the

Duck Pond

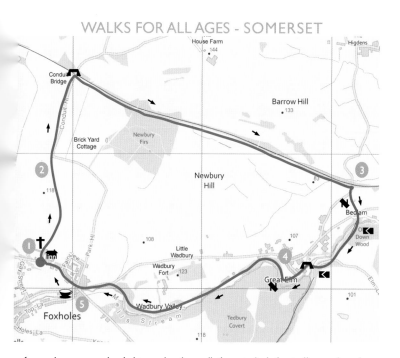

forges, hammers and grindstones by the early part of the nineteenth century. Around 1860 water power was replaced by steam to drive the machinery but after the demise of English agriculture around 1870 the Fussell family did not appear to react quickly enough to a changing marketplace, and the business was sold in 1894 to Isaac Nash, who after a short period closed the factory and auctioned off the machinery. Wildlife, and particularly horseshoe bats, have replaced the workers who previously toiled long and hard here.

5. Continuing along the footpath you come to a road where you turn left to enter the village of Mells. *** Continue to a junction where over on the left is a memorial by Lutyens to Mark Horner: a community water tap and shelter. Go ahead on the road, passing the post office/cafe on your right; taking care at

all times to look for traffic, as there is no footpath at this stage. Over on the left is a large 17th-century building, the Clothier's Mansion, and at the next junction there is more of Luytens' work, the War Memorial. Continue on, passing a fine 15th-century tithe barn in the yard on the left and now used as the village hall. Continue ahead until you reach the Talbot Inn.

*** An alternative route avoiding the road is to exit the footpath and turn left on the road and almost immediately follow the footpath sign on the right over a stone stile. Over the stile turn left and walk along the left edge of a field until you reach a house by an electricity pylon. Here you will find an exit onto a road and walk straight ahead until you reach kissing gate to field. This leads you to the field where you originally started your walk and you can walk back through the churchyard to New Street and the Talbot Inn.

NUNNEY CASTLE

A circular walk of 3 miles (5km) from the interesting village of Nunney. The village has a 14th-century moated castle. This easy circular walk starts in the village of Nunney and takes you through the village and along paths beside the Nunney Brook to open pastureland before returning back to the village.

Nunney is situated 3 miles (5km) from the town of Frome and 9 miles (15km) from Shepton Mallet off the A361. Parking is in the car park located just over the bridge in Castle Hill.

The beautiful historic village of Nunney was established on the wool and cloth industry.

Nunney Village

Market Cross

The name of the village comes from Old English and means "Nunna's Island". There are a number of weavers' cottages to be seen in the village as well as the village Guard House in Horn Street and the 15th-century George Inn. The Church of All Saints is a Grade I listed building and dates back to the 12th century.

For many years from the medieval period until the 19th century Nunney was the site of water-powered mills owned initially by the Hoddinotts and then by James Fussell. Fussell's iron works was well known thoughout Europe for its iron-edged farming tools. Once a year on the first Saturday in August the village streets are turned over to stalls of all kinds for a good old-fashioned Street Fayre.

Horse Jumps

Memorial Stone

Before you start the walk, or when you return, you can visit Nunney Castle, a fortified 14th-century castle which was the home of Sir John de la Mare, which he styled on the French castles he had seen whilst fighting in the Hundred Years War. The castle is moated and is now run by English Heritage as a tourist attraction and is a scheduled monument with free admission.

Nunney Brook

DONKEY LANE

THE BASICS

Distance in miles and km: 3miles (5km)

Gradient: Mostly level with one slight incline

Severity: Easy countryside walk

Approx min time to walk: 1hr 20mins

Stiles: No stiles

Maps: OS Explorer 142 Shepton Mallet and East Mendips

Path description: Riverside path, field paths and wooded track

Start Point: Public car park at Castle Hill GR 735 456

Parking: Public car park at Castle Hill GR 735 456

Dog friendly: On leads for preference

Public Toilets: None on route

Nearest food: George Inn, De La Mare Cafe, village shop

NUNNEY CASTLE WALK

1. Walk down from the car park to start the walk at the Market Place just over the bridge. Leave the Market Place and head along Church Street past the George Inn and then the village church on your right-hand side.

2. Continue past the Market Cross beside the Nunney Brook. This is an ideal spot to feed the ducks if you have children with you with any spare brown bread. A short

Nunney Castle

distance past the cross and before the road leaves the village you will find Donkey Lane on your left. Turn left into Donkey Lane and continue along the lane with a high wall on your left-hand side until you reach a gate and a footpath sign.

3. Continue ahead along a tree-lined drive towards Combe Farm until you reach a gate and kissing gate slightly to the right of the lane. Through the kissing gate continue along a wooded path and across an open grass area which contains a number of horse jumps. Note the horse jumps on the other side of the brook which are shaped as turtles. Nunney Brook is on your left and you should continue along the riverside path until you reach a footpath sign by a bridge.

4. Turn left onto the track over the river bridge and then immediately turn right by a footpath sign and stile. Follow this attractive riverside path with Nunney Brook on your right until the path then takes you up short slope to the left away from the brook to reach a gravel track.

5. Turn right and take the track over the bridge, following it as bends to the right towards a gate. Through the gate walk ahead as directed by a yellow footpath sign to a kissing gate which is hidden in the hedge to the left of a farm gate. Go through the kissing gate and follow a field path with the hedge on your right-hand side until at the end of the field you will reach a kissing gate.

6. Go through this kissing gate and follow a field path along the edge of field with the hedge on your left-hand side. As you walk along, look out for a hidden kissing gate in the hedge. Through this kissing gate turn right and follow the edge of the field to the corner and then continue along the edge of the field around to the left until you reach a gap at the corner of the field. Here you have interesting views towards the market town of Frome and Cley Hill in Wiltshire. Go through the gap and continue ahead slightly downhill to a further gap.

7. Turn right into the next field and cross the field diagonally right to a kissing gate ahead and pass through two kissing gates. Turn left and follow a field path

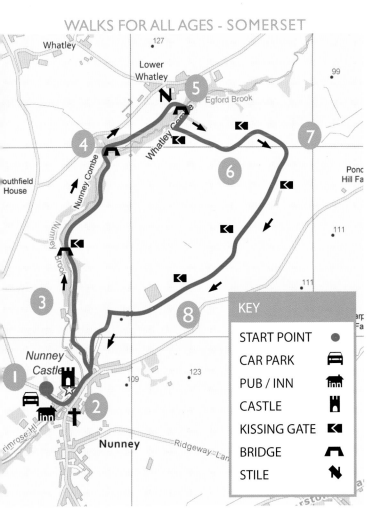

KEY

START POINT ●

CAR PARK 🚗

PUB / INN ⌂

CASTLE ♜

KISSING GATE ◄

BRIDGE ⌐

STILE ◣

around the edge of the field with the hedge on your left-hand side until you reach a farm gate and kissing gate in the corner of the field. Go through the kissing gate, turn right and follow the field path with the hedge on your right until you reach a farm gate and kissing gate. Through the kissing gate go across a farm track to a further kissing gate.

8. Follow the field path ahead until you reach another kissing gate which is situated slightly to your right. You now enter a beautiful enclosed tree-lined track which you follow and it takes you through two iron kissing gates before the track then becomes concrete and you pass houses on your left-hand side. You are now in Fulwell Lane, which leads into Donkey Lane. On reaching Donkey Lane turn left and follow the lane to reach Church Street. Turn right and then right again by the property called Praters, which takes you over a small bridge to visit Nunney Castle. On leaving the castle continue ahead along Castle Street to the road junction, turn right and now retrace your steps up Castle Hill to the car park.

WELLS

This historic circular walk of 3 miles (5km) around the beautiful city of Wells of will take 1½ hours. Wander around the beautiful city of Wells and learn about many of its ancient buildings.

There are plaques on some of the ancient buildings which will enable you to follow this tour of the city and you will be surprised by its beauty and ancient history.

Wells is located at the junction of three main roads: the A39 from Glastonbury to Bath, the A371 from Cheddar to Shepton Mallet and the B3139 which goes from Highbridge to Radstock. There are several car parks in the centre of the city.

Wells takes its name from the springs that rise from caverns in the grounds of the Bishop's Palace, which are known as St Andrew's Wells. In the 8th century the King of Wessex founded a minster church in Wells but there is evidence that the Romans also had a religious building near the site of the present cathedral.

The first evidence that there was a town in Wells was not until the 12th century and by 1180 the city's first charter had been granted. Wells continued to grow and became the largest town in Somerset by the 14th century. Manufacturing of cloth allowed the city to prosper, but with the decline in the 18th and early 19th century of the Somerset textile industry many towns lost their prosperity. Wells managed to survive these difficult times due to its ecclesiastical life and also to its development as a centre of genteel society.

Alms Houses

WELLS WALK.

1. Start the walk from outside the Town Hall in the Market Place. The building at one time housed the Law Courts. The row of buildings on the north side of the Market Place was built in 1451 by Bishop Bekynton. They were known as the New Works and backed onto the churchyard, against the 13th-century wall separating the Liberty from the town. The water from St Andrew's Well flows through the cellars of these houses. On the pavement in front of the shops is a memorial to the Olympic gold medal-winning jump of local athlete Mary Bignal Rand at the Tokyo Olympics in 1964. She was made a freeman of the City in 2012. Penniless Porch which adjoins New Works is also the work of Bishop Bekynton. It is one of two entrances into the Liberty from the Market Place.

2. You leave the Market Place through the Bishop's Eye, which is to the right of the National Trust shop. The Bishop's Eye is an imposing gateway leading to the Bishop's Palace. As you enter through the archway

Old City jail

THE BASICS

Distance in miles and km: 3 miles (5km)

Gradient: Flat walk

Severity: Easy city walk

Approx min time to walk: 1½ hours

Stiles: No stiles

Maps: OS Explorer 141 Cheddar Gorge & Mendip Hills West

Path description: Pavements and quiet roads

Start Point: Market Place GR 551 495

Parking: Several car parks in the City.

Dog friendly: On leads

Public Toilets: Union Street, Market Place

Nearest food: Various restaurants and cafes in city

2 Cont.

you see the moat and high defensive walls and gatehouse with a drawbridge and portcullis. These were built by Bishop Ralph of Shrewsbury in the 14th century and were a mark of his episcopal authority over the city. On the left of the gateway to the palace you will see a small rope with a bell. In the 19th century the daughter of the Bishop taught a swan to ring the bell to be fed. This tradition continues to this day and the swan is very much synonymous with Wells. The Bishop of Bath and Wells still resides in part of the Palace. The Palace is open to the public. Follow the path alongside the moat towards the fields. On your right you will see the recreation ground which was given to the people of Wells in celebration of Queen Victoria's Golden Jubilee of 1887. On the edge of the recreation ground is the 15th-century Bishop's Tithe Barn. There is also evidence here that there was once a rabbit warren on the edge of the Bishop's deer park in the 13th century.

Wells Tythe Barn

3. Continue around the moat until you see on your left water rushing over the weir from the Bishop's Garden. Four million gallons of water comes from the wells each day. In 1451 a well house was built by Bishop Bekynton and lead pipes were laid to carry water to the Market Place and the Palace. You now retrace your steps back along the moat and back through the Bishop's Eye and turn right and right again through Penniless Porch and onto Cathedral Green.

Bishop's Palace Moat

4. In front of you is the West Front of the Cathedral which was started by Bishop Reginald de Bohun in 1180. By 1508 the building of the cathedral and the cloisters was complete. The entrance to the cathedral is to the right of the West Front. Now walk across Cathedral Green to the road and turn right. In this road is the 15th-century Deanery and a little further along is Wells Museum, which was once the house of the Chancellor and houses important collections of finds from caves on the Mendips, including the witch of Wookey Hole, together with the story of how the Mendip Hills were formed. Outside the Museum is a memorial stone to Harry Patch, the last fighting soldier of World War I, who spent his later years in a residential home in Wells. The old Archdeaconry is next to the museum and is now the music school of Wells Cathedral School. Continue ahead

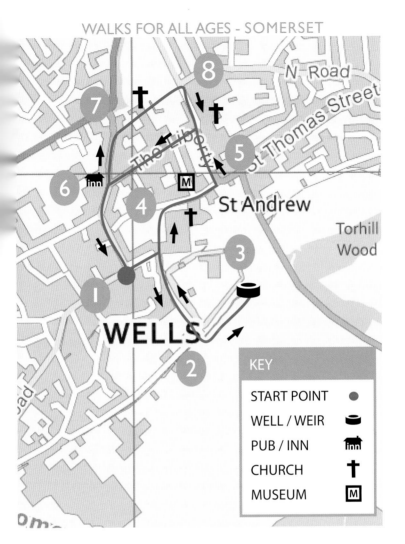

KEY

START POINT	●
WELL / WEIR	⬭
PUB / INN	🏠
CHURCH	✝
MUSEUM	Ⓜ

and under another beautiful archway, the Chain Gate Bridge, which joins the cathedral and provided the Vicars with a way into the cathedral and away from worldly temptations. Turn left into Vicars Close, which was built in 1363 by Bishop Ralph of Shrewsbury to house the Vicars Choral. The first building in the close was a communal dining hall which was used until 1592. Administrative buildings were added in the early 15th century including an exchequer, muniment room and a treasury. This street is the oldest

continuously inhabited street in Europe still being used for its original purpose to house the Vicars Choral. At the top of the close is the Vicar's Chapel and Liberty, which is well worth a visit.

5. Walk back down Vicars Close and into St Andrew Street and note the 15th-century Rib on your right, which is the only serving house of three which were a gift of the Bishop and were known as the Bishop's Ribs and was for some time the home of the Cathedral School's

headmaster and previously the principal of the old Theological College. Continue to the pedestrian crossing and cross the road, turn left and walk along the East Liberty. There are many imposing houses in the Liberty and these are now part of the Cathedral School. You continue along East Liberty and then turn left into North Liberty, then left into New Street and then left again into Sadler Street. You pass the Ancient Gatehouse Hotel and Brown's Gatehouse on your left with the Swan Hotel on the right. The Swan Hotel was mentioned in city records dating back to 1422.

6. Walk down Sadler Street to the corner of the Market Place. Here you will find the conduit which was built in the late 18th century and replaced the medieval one which was built by Bishop Bekynton. Now turn right and walk down the High Street until you reach a Y-junction. Take the right-hand road, passing the City Arms Inn on your left which is on the corner of Queens Street. The City Arms Inn was both an inn and a gaol in the 16th century and some of the cells still exist.

7. Continue to the corner of Priest Row with St Cuthbert's Church ahead. St Cuthbert's is the largest parish church in Somerset. It was built mainly in the 14th and 15th centuries and inside the church it has a magnificent painted ceiling. At the rear of the church you will find the beautiful Walter Bricke Almshouses which were built in the 17th century. Continue along Priest Row, and on your left is another set of almshouses known as the Still Almshouses which were built by Bishop Still in 1640, and also the Llewellyn Almshouses which were bequeathed by Henry Llewellyn, who left £1,600 for the almshouses to be built for ten elderly women of the parish. Continue until you reach the junction at Chamberlain Street and turn left. Walk a little way along and on your right you will see the Bubwith's Almshouses which were a gift of Bishop Bubwith in the early 15th century. They were to provide accommodation for twelve men and women who were burgesses of the city.

Vicars Close

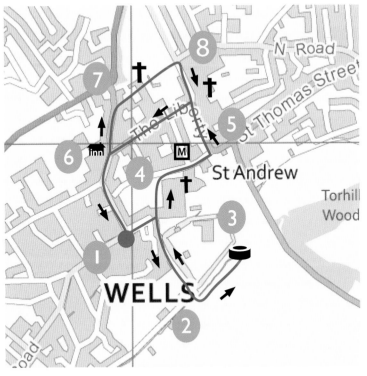

8. Retrace your steps back and walk up Chamberlain Street and on the left-hand side you will see Elim Church, which was used temporarily as a convent by Carmelite nuns and was brought in 1937 to be used as an Elim tabernacle. On the right-hand side you will pass the Roman Catholic Church of St Joseph and St Teresa. In 1875 Carmelite nuns came to Wells from Plymouth and were installed in a house now called Chamberlain House. Continue along Chamberlain Street until you reach the junction with Sadler Street, turn right into Sadler Street and then left back into the Market Place to complete your tour of Wells.

WOOKEY HOLE

A choice of two walks: one of 6miles (10km) which is a circular walk and a shorter walk of 4 miles (6.5km) which is linear and you return by the same route.

These two walks start from the centre of the city of Wells and take you through the town and out into the countryside of the Mendip Hills. The longer circular route takes you up onto the hills, where there are magnificent views of the Somerset Levels and Glastonbury Tor and the Quantocks in the distance.

The route then takes you through Ebbor Gorge Nature Reserve and down into the village of Wookey Hole, famous for the Wookey Hole Caves. In wet weather the tracks can be muddy in places.

The shorter route follows the longer route into the countryside but doesn't take you high onto the Mendip Hills.

Wookey Hole Inn

Wells is located at the junction of three main roads: the A39 from Glastonbury to Bath, the A371 from Cheddar to Shepton Mallet and the B3139 which goes from Highbridge to Radstock. There are several car parks in the centre of the city.

Wells is the smallest city in England and has a most magnificent cathedral (see also Walk 18). The wells, which gave the city its name, are located within the grounds of the Bishop's Palace, which is still the residence of the Bishop of Bath and Wells. The moated Bishop's Palace dates from the early 13th century when Bishop Jocelin Trotman, the first Bishop to hold the title Bishop of Bath and Wells, received a crown licence to build a residence and deer park on land to the south of the Cathedral of St Andrew.

The Mendip Hills stretch from Frome in the east of Somerset to Weston-super-Mare in the West. It is made up of carboniferous limestone which is porous, therefore allowing the water to percolate through the rock, and over millions of years

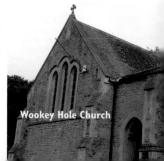
Wookey Hole Church

caves have been formed underground. The most well-known of these are Cheddar Caves and Wookey Hole.

Wookey Hole Caves have been a source of wonder to visitors since Roman times. Carved under the beautiful Mendip Hills by the River Axe the first known record was in the third century AD. The caves have attracted visitors for many centuries but it is only since 1927, when electricity was introduced and stairways built, that they have been open to visitors. There are 25 explored caverns with exploration and discovery of new caverns still taking place. The mill at Wookey Hole has long been part of the village. Originally a corn mill and then a cloth mill, it has also been a paper mill. The mill and the caves are open to the public.

Old Lime Kilns

THE BASICS

Distance in miles and km: 6 miles or 4 miles (10km or 6.5km)

Gradient: Undulating. The longer walk has steeper climbs.

Severity: Moderate, with steeper climbs

Approx min time to walk: 3 hours or 1½ hours

Stiles: Four stiles on longer route. None on short route,

Maps: OS Explorer 141 Cheddar Gorge & Mendip Hills West

Path description: Tracks and field paths can be muddy on longer walk

Start Point: Market Place GR 551 495

Parking: Several car parks in the city

Dog friendly: On leads

Public Toilets: Union Street , Market Place

Nearest food: Various restaurants and cafes in city

WOOKEY HOLE WALK

1. Leave the Market Place and turn right into Sadler Street past the Swan Hotel/White Hart Hotel to reach New Street, where you turn right and take the left-hand footpath and after a short distance (by a red postbox) you will find a West Mendip Way marker post, at which you turn left. Proceed along, bearing right, and then turn left into Lovers Walk and continue along to take the footbridge over the main road to enter the grounds of Wells Blue School. Continue through the grounds and exit the school by some buildings and continue along a tarmac path through a field to a road.

2. Cross the road and on the other side of the road you will find a narrow lane between houses. Climbing steadily, you reach another road which you cross over to join the footpath again to a further road, where you again cross and continue upwards through a kissing gate to reach a waymark stating "Wookey Hole 1.5 miles". Here you join a minor road and follow this road left, with the old Underwood Quarry on your left, behind the hedge. A rift was found in Underwood Quarry in 1937 and among the items identified were the bones of 150,000-year-old deer, hippopotamus and other bovine animals. These can be seen in Wells Museum, located opposite the Cathedral.
***For shorter walk see end.

3. Ignoring any left or right turns, continue straight ahead on a short tree-lined grassy track to a kissing gate and field gate.

Go through the kissing gate, bear right across a field to find, on the left of a farmhouse, a kissing gate to another field, where you go downhill to cross a stream and pass through a further kissing gate. Follow the path up with the hedge on your left to the top of the ridge and down, bearing right to another kissing gate. Continue across the field, aiming for a wooden stile in the top left-hand corner, which leads you onto a minor road (Milton Lane).

4. Turn left on the road and almost immediately on the right take the second metal gate (opposite Lower Milton Farm Cottages) and follow a track up close to the right-hand hedge to a further gate. Continue the steady climb, always following the track, through a further gate until you reach a stile/metal gate with waymark signs, to enter a wood. Continue along the stony track to a further gate. The track bears right and now becomes more of a path and leads up to a further stile/gate. All the time there are wonderful views of the Somerset Levels and the Quantocks in the distance.

5. Climb over the stile and the path now disappears. Walk up the field and look for a stile/gate in the hedge on your left on the brow of the hill. Cross over the stile and continue straight ahead, following the line of the hedge to reach a further stile (ignore the metal stile on the right), while taking time out to enjoy the wonderful views. After crossing the

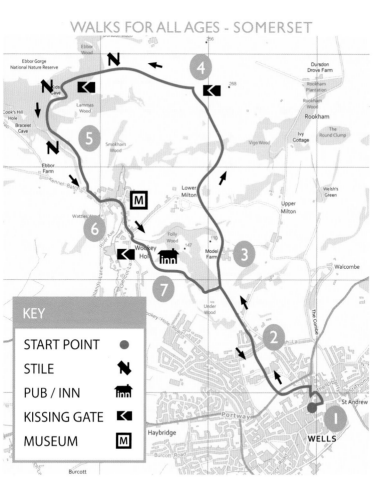

KEY

START POINT	●
STILE	↖
PUB / INN	🏠
KISSING GATE	◄
MUSEUM	Ⓜ

stile you will see a gate straight ahead with a waymark to the left. Bearing left, walk towards the fence. Continuing left with the wire fence now on your right-hand side and continue downhill to a wooden signpost with a gate and stile with the path entering Ebbor Gorge Nature Reserve. Follow the track down to a further stile onto the main stony track through beautiful woodland. At a crossing of tracks continue straight ahead until you see a "Cliff Edge'" caution sign, where you have the opportunity to enjoy one of the most spectacular views in Somerset from the rock of Ebbor Slaits. Ebbor Gorge was formed in the Ice

Age and was once a vast cave, the roof of which was gradually worn away over millions of years. The caves were the home for deer and lemming but now are a home for colonies of bats.

6. Leave Ebbor Slaits by retracing your steps and take the first track to your right following the "West Mendip Way" sign to the right down a footpath with numerous steps until you reach a wide track at the foot of the Gorge. Here you turn left (waymarked "Wookey Hole") and continue along the track to reach a gate and stile and nature reserve information board. Follow the track over the stile and continue

along what is often a muddy valley to reach a kissing gate and road. You are now in Wookey Hole village. Turn left on the road and continue along to reach the centre of the village and the entrance to Wookey Hole Caves and Paper Mill, which you may wish to visit.

7. The village has a number of places to take refreshment. However, to resume the walk you continue along the road, passing the Wookey Hole Inn and ignoring the first turning on the left (Milton Lane). Ccontinue ahead a short distance to find on the left-hand side a kissing gate by a waymark into a field. Go through the gate and follow the field path with the hedge on your right to a further kissing gate and then along a narrow path to another kissing gate. This gate leads to a minor road where you turn left and continue uphill along the road until you come to a metal gate and kissing gate. As you progress along the road on your left-hand side just behind some bushes you will see two old lime kilns. You will have passed Underwood Quarry again on your right. Turn right and follow the lane to junction and turn right. You are on the same path through the houses as your outward route. Follow the route back through the school and over the road bridge and back to the Market Place.

*** Shorter Walk: As the road bends to its right and with the footpath marker on your left, turn left through a metal gate and continue ahead on the road passing some old lime kilns just off the road along a short track to your right. If you have stopped to look at the kilns return to the road and continue along until you reach a kissing gate on your right. Go through the kissing gate and on to a further gate before entering a field. Continue ahead along the field with the hedge on your left to reach a further kissing gate and road. Turn right to enter the village of Wookey Hole. Continue along the road, passing Wookey Hole Inn on your right, and then you reach the old Mill and the Wookey Hole Caves. To return, reverse your route out of the village and back to Wells.

KING ALFRED'S TOWER

An easy 4-mile (6.5km) circular walk suitable for all the family. This walk is on the Stourhead Estate and takes you from King Alfred's Tower along forest tracks and across open countryside.

The route is mostly along the old "Carriage Way" used by the owners of Stourhead House in days gone by.

Parking is at King Alfred's Tower in the National Trust woodland car park on a minor road off the B3092 from Frome.

King Alfred's Tower was built in 1772 and stands on the border of the counties of Somerset, Wiltshire and Dorset and at 160 feet (49m) high is reputedly one of the tallest follies in Britain. It stands on the point where King Alfred the Great was thought to have rallied his troops in AD 878 before the Battle of Edington.

Stourhead House

The tower is now owned by the National Trust and you are able to climb the two hundred and five steps to the top of the tower. From the top of the tower you have wonderful views across the three counties.

The Stourhead Estate of 2,650 acres is now owned and managed by the National Trust and was given to the Trust in 1945 by the Hoare family. The famous gardens were designed by Henry Hoare II and laid out between 1741 and 1780 in a classical 18th-century design set around a large lake, achieved by damming a small stream. Included in the garden are a number of temples inspired by scenes of the Grand Tour of Europe.

On one hill overlooking the gardens there stands an obelisk and King Alfred's Tower, while on another hill the temple of Apollo provides a vantage point to survey the magnificent rhododendrons, water cascades and

Arch into Village

temples. The large medieval Bristol High Cross was moved from Bristol to the gardens. Stourhead House was one of the first country villas to be built in the new Palladian style and was designed by Colen Campbell for Henry Hoare I, who unfortunately died the same year in which the house was completed. Amongst the hills surrounding the estate there are also two Iron Age hill forts

Manor gate

The Lodge

The Tower

THE BASICS

Distance in miles and km: 4 miles (6.5km)

Gradient: Small undulations

Severity: Easy walking

Approx min time to walk: 2 hours

Stiles: No stiles

Maps: Explorer 142 Mendip Hills East

Path description: Forest track and field paths

Start Point: King Alfred's Tower GR 745 350

Parking: at King Alfred's Tower on minor road off the B3092 from Frome.

Dog friendly: On leads

Public Toilets: Stourhead Amenities

Nearest food: National Trust Restaurant, Spread Eagle Inn

KING ALFRED'S TOWER WALK

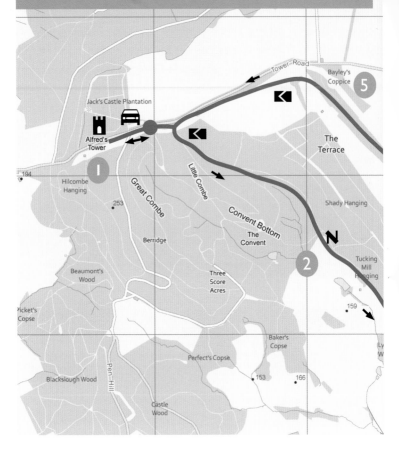

1. You start the walk by leaving the car park and crossing the road and entering an open grass area. King Alfred's Tower is to your right. After visiting the Tower, retrace your steps back the way you have come and then turn down the third track on the right, signified by a fingerpost footpath sign. The track takes you initially downhill and undulates through the woods and you continue on the main track, ignoring any left or right turns, until you reach a gate and stile.

2. Go through the gate and into the field and continue in the same direction, passing through a gate to a track, which you continue to follow in the direction of Turners Paddock.

Pass through a further gate with a stile and follow a track through a field with Beech Cottage on your left. Wind your way down, passing a signpost for Stourton, to a further gate. You are now walking with one lake above you and one below to reach a road. Turn left on the road passing under a rock arch. This peculiar structure, humped over a narrow lane, was built from knobbly tufa rock imported from Italy.

3. You are now in the village of Stourton, with the entrance to the famous gardens on your left. Pass the parish church of St Peter and turn right into the courtyard of the Spread Eagle Inn and cross the courtyard

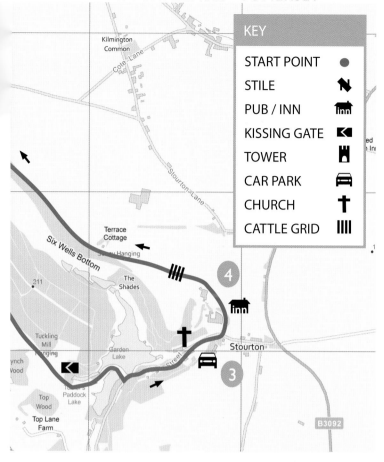

under the archway between shops. Follow the path ahead up towards the Stourhead reception area, but when the path bears around to the right go left along the path to meet a road. If you wish to visit the Stourhead Visitor Centre, restaurant and shop you will need to continue on the path and not go to your left.

4. Cross the road and go through the ancient gateway and continue along the driveway passing in front of Stourhead House to a cattle grid and gate. Go through the gate, turning left to follow the "Carriage Way". Continue to follow this wide track, passing through a gate to the next field where

you will see an obelisk, which was originally erected in 1746 and rebuilt in 1839. Continue along, passing through two gates, with Terrace Lodge house on your right. You have now entered the Terrace and should continue to follow this walk for around half a mile (1km) to another gate.

5. Pass through the gate and follow the field as it bears left at the top and shortly you can look down the valley of Six Wells Bottom on your left, where you can find the source of the River Stour. Continue along the ridge, passing through a gate, and then continue along in same direction and after a further half a mile (1km) you will arrive back at Alfred's Tower.

91

MARTOCK

An easy circular walk of 3¾ miles (6km) from the village of Martock. This easy, undulating walk takes you from the historic village of Martock, passing many beautiful buildings, across open countryside with wonderful views of South Petherton and the River Parrett Valley.

The picturesque village of Martock is well worth exploring with its many blue plaque buildings, shops, pubs and cafes.

Parking is in the village at the Martock Recreation Ground off Stoke Lane. The village lies 7 miles (11km) north-west of Yeovil off the A303.

Martock, together with Hurst and Bower Hinton, forms a long village between the Rivers Isle and Parrett. It was once a centre of commerce and industry and is now a haven for arts, crafts and heritage. The name Martock comes from the Old English words "mart" meaning market and "ac" for oak and relate to an oak tree on the spot now occupied by the Market House.

Martock's many attractive and historic buildings are constructed in stone from the nearby Ham Hill. This golden sedimentary Hamstone lends a mellow warmth to the buildings, some of which date back to the medieval period.

In the 16th and 17th centuries, Martock enjoyed a period of great prosperity, due to the fertile local soils and good farming practices. By the 18th and early 19th centuries it was the clothing and glove-making trades that created wealth for the village. Manufacturing developed with the opening of the Parrett works. The Parrett Iron Works was a series of industrial buildings next to the River Parrett.

Village Centre

The site was originally named Carey's Mill and the adjoining bridge is called Carey's Mill Bridge, which was built of Hamstone in the 18th century. The Iron Works was founded in 1855, on the site of a former snuff mill. The site included a foundry, with a prominent chimney, ropewalk, workshops and several smaller workshops and cottages. The sluice which powered the waterwheel and sluice keepers' cottage still exist.

The River Parrett is 37 miles (60km) long and its source is in the hills around Chedington, Dorset. It then flows north-west through Somerset and the Somerset Levels to its mouth at Burnham-on-Sea and into the Bristol Channel.

Parrett Works

THE BASICS

Distance in miles and km: 3 ¾ miles (6km)

Gradient: Undulating

Severity: Easy walking

Approx min time to walk: 2 hours

Stiles: 5

Maps: OS Explorer 129 Yeovil

Path description: Field paths, farm tracks, country roads

Start Point: Martock Recreation Ground GR 463 192

Parking: Martock Recreation Ground GR 463 192

Dog friendly: On leads

Public Toilets: Martock village

Nearest food: Pubs and cafe in village

MARTOCK WALK

1. From the car park in the Recreation Ground, head across the playing field towards a tall row of poplar trees. To the right of the trees join a gravel track which you follow across further playing fields. As the track bends to the right take the track to the left between hedges, passing a kissing gate on your left, and continue to the end of the track to reach a gate. Go through the gate and turn right and continue along the track, passing houses and eventually meeting a road. Turn left and walk along the pavement passing The Hollies hotel on your left, until you reach an open green on the right and cross over the road into Middle Street.

2. Walk along Middle Street until you come to a road junction. Turn left into Back Lane and walk along this interesting street, and as the road bends around to the left continue along Back Lane, passing the historic 13th-century Bower Hinton Farm. You leave the road and join a track which takes you to gate and stile. After 20 yards (20m) turn right and follow the track straight ahead at a crossroad of tracks and continue ahead following farm track through several fields over Cripple Hill, with wonderful views of South Petherton and beyond. The track descends down to a hedge and direction post.

3. Turn left and walk along a field path with the hedge on your right to a stile in the hedge on your right. Cross over the stile and head across the field to a gap in the hedge and a sleeper across the ditch. Turn left and follow a path between hedges, turning right and crossing a wooden bridge and then on to a further metal bridge crossing the River Parrett. Keeping right, follow the path along the banks of the River Parrett, crossing a stile, and then leave the river bank to follow a path towards a stile in the hedge. Cross over the stile and continue down the field with the hedge on your left, aiming for and passing stable buildings on your right, and through a further gate and two metal stiles to meet the road.

4. On reaching the road turn right and walk along the road to the Parrett Works, passing "Kellys Yard" and "Castle Reclamation" to find a fingerpost between a stone wall and bungalow on the right. Through the gate follow the track to a gate, stile and hedge. Take the small gate to your left and follow the path between fences to a further gate and then along the field path with the hedge on your right to a small gate and bridge. Keep left and walk with the hedge on your left to a small gate and then on to a further gate and track. Turn left and follow the track to a road.

5. On reaching the road turn right and continue along the road until you reach a fingerpost and metal bridge on your left.

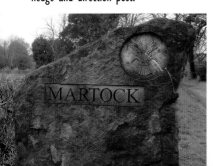

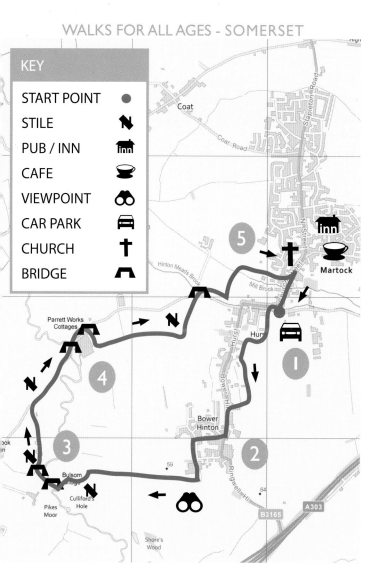

KEY

START POINT	●
STILE	⋏
PUB / INN	🏠
CAFE	☕
VIEWPOINT	👓
CAR PARK	🚗
CHURCH	†
BRIDGE	⌒

Walk across a field to a gate opposite and then turn right and follow the path to a metal bridge. Cross over the bridge and, keeping right, follow the edge of the field towards Martock's All Saints Church and field gate. Turn right and follow Pound Lane with Martock churchyard wall on your left to reach the village. Here you may wish to spend some time exploring this interesting village with its many historic buildings, shops, pubs and cafes. To return to the car park turn right and follow the road to the junction and cross over the road into Stoke Lane, and the Martock Recreation Ground is on your right.

ABOUT THE AUTHOR

Together with my husband Graham, I have been running a walking holiday company for 14 years since our retirement from our professional careers and it has been with great pleasure that I have been able to bring together this book of walks for all the family.

Through writing this book of walks it has been an opportunity for me to inform more people of how beautiful and interesting the county of Somerset is and for those who live in Somerset perhaps a chance to discover new places to take the family.

The book is also for my Grandchildren whom I hope will join me on a few walks when they come to visit and they too will come to enjoy the diversity and beauty of Somerset. Enjoy the countryside and your walking.

Sue Robinson.

www.bathwestwalks.com